MILLENNIUM

FENTRESS BRADBURN
Selected and Current Works

FENTRESS BRADBURN
Selected and Current Works

MILLENNIUM

First published in Australia in 2001 by
The Images Publishing Group Pty Ltd
ACN 059 734 431
6 Bastow Place, Mulgrave, Victoria 3170
Telephone (61 3) 9561 5544 Facsimile (61 3) 9561 4860
E-mail: books@images.com.au

Copyright © The Images Publishing Group Pty Ltd 2001

All rights reserved. Apart from any fair dealing
for the purposes of private study, research,
criticism or review as permitted under the Copyright Act,
no part of this publication may be reproduced,
stored in a retrieval system or transmitted in
any form by any means, electronic, mechanical,
photocopying or otherwise, without the
written permission of the publisher.

National Library of Australia Cataloguing-in-Publication data

Fentress Bradburn: selected and current works.

Bibliography.
Includes index.
ISBN 1 876907 12 6.

1. Fentress Bradburn (Firm) 2. Architecture, American.
3. Architecture, Modern – 20th century – United States.
(Series: Millennium (Mulgrave, Vic.).)

720.973

Edited by Renée Otmar, Otmar Miller Consultancy Pty Ltd, Melbourne
Designed by The Graphic Image Studio Pty Ltd, Mulgrave, Australia
Printed by Everbest Printing Co. Ltd., China

Contents

9   Preface *by Curtis Worth Fentress*

11 Introduction *by John Morris Dixon*

Selected and Current Works

Recent Works

18   Seoul Inchon International Airport Passenger Terminal

34   Regional Transportation Commission and Regional Flood Control District Headquarters

42   Kuwait Finance House Tower

46   Colorado Convention Center Expansion

52   David E. Skaggs Federal Building

62   Seattle-Tacoma International Airport Central Terminal Expansion

68   Loveland Police and Courts Building

70   Colorado State Capitol Life-Safety Renovation

74   421 Broadway Renovation/Expansion

78   Complex Suria Merdeka

80   Research Complex I

88   Cherry Hills Community Church Chapel

90   J.D. Edwards & Co. Corporate Campus

Competitions

96   Clark County Government Center

112   Natural Resources Building

118   Larimer County Justice Center

124   Civic Center Parking Structure

126   La Nueva Área Terminal del Aeropuerto Madrid/Barajas

132   Flughafen Wien

134   The Hughes Center

142   The AEC Design Competition 1996

144   Cathedral City Civic Center

Contents continued

Special Projects

150 National Museum of Wildlife Art

166 Denver International Airport Passenger Terminal

176 The Denver Permit Center

180 The Tritch Building Renovation and The Rialto Café

184 Temple Sinai

188 Palmetto Bay Beach Resort

192 IBM Customer Service Center

196 The Balboa Company Corporate Headquarters

198 Gulf Canada Resources Ltd

Design

202 The Birdhouse Project 1998

204 ICE Terminal Köln-Deutz/Messe

206 Sacramento High Rise Lot A

208 Terminal 2, Flughafen München

212 Dinosaur Discovery Museum

214 Colorado History Museum Expansion

216 Central California History Museum

220 Colorado Christian University

Firm Profile

227 Associates and Collaborators

229 Selected Competitions

230 Selected Awards

232 Chronological List of Buildings, Projects and Credits

250 Selected Bibliography

252 Acknowledgments

253 Index

Preface

Making It Material
Curtis Worth Fentress, FAIA

I have always worked from instinct and have been guided by intuition. The connections I have made throughout almost 30 years of practising architecture have been the product of an intuitive process, one by which I have not only chosen the projects to pursue and the main thrust of our designs, but also the people with whom I've surrounded myself.

I am someone who relies on analysis—but only as the basis for intuitive assessment. In all matters, the "feel" of a person, place, thing or situation is paramount for me. And for me, the practice of architecture is the business of creating that "feel" for other people.

Theory comes out of practice, not the other way around. Intuition has always guided me; it is only afterward, on reflection, that it is possible to see what principles were upheld by such intuitive choices. This can be frightening territory—it can seem capricious and random; one is sustained only by faith in one's judgment. Now, with many years of work behind me, it is easy to see the threads common to the wide diversity of projects we have undertaken.

Designing for region and context—hallmarks of Fentress Bradburn's work—seem to me to be a corollary of our intuitive approach. One cannot get a sense for a place and the people who live there without relating to the environs, whether that constitutes landforms, customs, culture, community or the nature of the work that will be done inside the structure. One cannot listen to a client, a board of directors or an entire community and not sense the need to ground a building in what already exists, to harmonize with the landscape and the built environment, as well as the driving force of those who will live with the building. Buildings are about people, and people do not exist in a vacuum or in an artistic ether that is inaccessible to others. We had to "know" the desert and the people of Clark County before creating a vessel for their governance. Experiencing Korean temples and learning about royal processions helped us fashion Seoul Inchon International Airport in a way that embraces the traveler. Negotiating between the scientists of the National Oceanic and Atmospheric Administration's Boulder Research Labs and the community that surrounded the site ensured that the David E. Skaggs Federal Building was a structure that served everyone.

Given our intuitive approach and the significance of region and context for us, people's comfort is a primary concern of our work. But this is not just a matter of creating pleasant spaces or ensuring short walks to baggage claim or making a civic building easy to navigate. The kind of comfort I mean is a deeper quality. It is about feeling at home in the world, something increasingly rare in a time of such mind-boggling change. This has always been my mission: to figure out what it means in any given situation to make people feel at home with a structure—and then to make that feeling material.

For me, the first step in that process is to get a feeling for the place and the people. The touch of clay to the architect's hand, as it were, may come in walking the site or in visiting a culture's most revered and most ordinary sites. It may come in a conversation, an aside, a pained look or a passionate outburst in a public meeting. But this is the true raw material from which great architecture springs, the stuff of human desires and fears and needs and wants. Design is an alchemy that begins with the wish for a new structure and is fed not just by the architect's imagination but by people and by what they already know, even if only subconsciously, about what will make them comfortable in the deepest possible sense of that word.

This is what sustains us through scores of public meetings and the difficulties of creating structures on foreign shores: that there will come a moment when we will hear or see or somehow come into contact with what is deepest in the heart of a client—what is in fact the soul of a building that has yet to be created. I believe that it is only by intuition that one can grasp this. Theory does not serve here; movements or styles cannot receive or respond to this information. For me, instinct and intuition are the guiding forces by which it is possible to perceive this quality of comfort, and to make it material.

Introduction

High Goals on the High Plains
John Morris Dixon, FAIA

Denver is a city of strong contrasts. The Great Plains stretch westward for hundreds of miles, becoming higher and emptier, until at this point they collide with the Rocky Mountains. The metropolis that grew at that crucial boundary has two aspects, as well. It is in many respects a no-nonsense business center of a vast region, now boasting non-stop flights to Europe. Yet, the sight of the mountains constantly reminds Denver residents of a world of skiing and fishing, of campfires and potential solitude. It's possible to become career-driven here, of course, but harder than in New York or Chicago.

In the area of architecture, Denver has always had a few firms with recognition and commissions outside Colorado, but Fentress Bradburn is the first to design anything like a 6-million-square-foot airport in Asia. Meanwhile, the firm has been shaping the most prominent landmarks in Denver: that city's dramatic airport terminal, its convention center, and a new professional football stadium at the edge of downtown (designed in association with HNTB Sports). And beyond Denver, these architects' skills are evident in an amazing variety of works: airports, government centers, laboratories, museums, office buildings, office interiors—even a tropical resort.

Fentress Bradburn has succeeded in transplanting the scope and ambitions of a major East Coast firm to the foot of the Rockies. Like any transplant, this one has had to adapt to the outdoors-oriented culture of Denver and to being located where the world does not expect an international contender.

The key adaptive strategy that has made Fentress Bradburn an internationally known firm is its dedication to design competitions. While most large, established firms avoid design competitions—even if they owe their early successes to them—Fentress Bradburn remains eager to enter them. After getting an early boost by winning the Colorado Convention Center competition, the firm has entered many more (nine of them are covered in this book), including the contest for that big Asian project, the air gateway to Korea.

The competition-winning designs demonstrate the distinguishing principles of the firm's output. They never do anything outlandish—as architects are tempted to do—to win a competition. Their competition schemes are scrupulously thought-out responses to the clients' briefs, with forms that are striking and memorable but firmly grounded in the place and function, so that they earn the local support essential to getting winning designs built.

One principle underpinning their design is that no consistent look is imposed. The firm's buildings are extremely divergent, depending on place and purpose. In large-scale works such as the airports, the architecture often is based on a

1

2

1 New Bronco Stadium against the horizon, existing stadium at right
2 Stadium, construction shot

dramatic structural concept. But whatever the scale, the buildings express the character of the place—in local traditions and materials, in subtle adjustments in their prominence in the landscape or the urban scene. The Denver airport celebrates advanced technology because that's the essence of air travel, and it proclaims its immense importance on this flat landscape with a silhouette that echoes that of the mountains. The National Museum of Wildlife Art, on the other hand, blends into the local outcroppings as thoroughly as an ancient Native American ruin.

Whatever the images the buildings project, their designs are founded on the experience of the users. Though that experience starts with the initial image, which is crucial, it involves as well the entrances, the sequence of exterior and interior spaces, the clarity and interest of internal paths, the suitability of various rooms to their roles. In many of their buildings, the form and technology of the structure is exceptional, but the ultimate goal of it all, say the partners, is "the physical and psychological comfort of the end-user."

3   Lobby, Denver Center Theater (Roche Dinkeloo)
4   Amoco Building, Denver (Kohn Pedersen Fox)

Getting to this point

From the day they established their firm in 1980, founding partners Curtis Worth Fentress and James Henry Bradburn were ready to take on big commissions. Both had come to Denver to work on major projects for firms accustomed to handling such projects. Fentress had come here for the construction phase of the prominent Amoco Tower by the New York firm of Kohn Pedersen Fox Associates, after playing a major role in the building's design. Bradburn had similarly come to Denver to represent the internationally respected Connecticut firm of Roche Dinkeloo, in the realization of the Denver Center for the Performing Arts.

In skills and personalities, the two meshed in the ways in which so many effective architectural partnerships always have. Fentress is the design leader—these days as often the design critic or design nurturer as the actual designer—a high-energy, highly verbal person. Bradburn supplies the special expertise to support new and unusual design concepts, seeing to the execution of design documents and construction with quiet assurance. Complementary in so many ways, the two principals also have critical similarities in their optimism and their high aspirations.

Curt Fentress had worked for five years at the I.M. Pei firm, then had been the sixth architect to join Kohn Pedersen Fox, shortly after its founding in 1976. He had seen that firm (whose founders had also arrived with big-firm experience) quickly win large, geographically dispersed commissions. He fondly recalls the ferment of architectural ideas in New York at that time, generated by events at the Institute for Architecture and Urban Studies and by lectures at Columbia University. Yet, a few years older, with a more settled home life in Denver, he decided not to return to New York. Jim Bradburn had been a protégé of John Dinkeloo, an architect known for carrying out the virtuoso structural systems and

Introduction 13

detailing of Roche Dinkeloo's widespread, highly visible works. A person more attracted to open spaces than bright lights, Bradburn also decided to stay in Denver. By their great good fortune, the two got together.

The partners' intentions, says Fentress, were to "start a firm that could do buildings of the quality of the firms we had worked for—but from Denver." Though usually the low-keyed partner, Bradburn recalls that initial goal as even more ambitious, saying the quality of their previous firms' work was "a minimum standard. We had to go on from there."

In architectural practice, of course, readiness to take on challenging work does not bring it to your door. "Being from New York was a plus," Fentress recalls, in a city that had been looking to the East Coast for design of its major buildings. And the partners had gotten to know who was who in Denver. Their first commissions were for developer office buildings, on the outskirts of the city, and office buildings still represent a large proportion of their practice. A major step for the fledgling practice was winning the commission in 1981 for the 1999 Broadway office building, a 44-story tower in the heart of downtown Denver, which is notable for its compatibility with a fine old church that shares its city block.

The firm's ticket to even larger, more visible and diverse work was their winning entry in the 1987 design competition for the Colorado Convention Center in Denver. This $125-million project catapulted them into another league. Here, they competed with numerous firms, including I.M. Pei & Partners, and prevailed. (Now, they have completed plans to double the center's size, while thoroughly remodeling the original structure—a commission won without a design competition, on the basis of their earlier accomplishment here.)

The next big jump in scale was designing the Denver International Airport (1991–94), a $455-million project that came their way in stages. Having proved at the Convention Center its ability to deliver large projects on time and within budget, Fentress Bradburn was originally commissioned to be the architect of record to follow the out-of-town firm, Perez, chosen to design the airport. When that firm's scheme turned out to be $75 million over budget (and "not memorable," according to Denver's mayor at the time), Fentress Bradburn was asked to step in as the designer and re-design to meet the budget. They were also invited to propose an alternative concept of their own—if they could present it convincingly in three weeks! The response to that challenge: the bravura fabric structure that made the budget work and has come to be Denver's signature landmark.

Completion of such a major airport terminal opened up opportunities in a field with few competitors worldwide. As Fentress explains, however, a chance to do a second airport comes only after the five or six years it takes to get the first airport built and operating. And, by then, you have to meet new expectations in this rapidly evolving area. The firm has since been invited to enter five design competitions for airports, losing two (Bangkok and Madrid), winning two (Seoul, Korea, and Doha, Qatar), and earning honorable mention in another (Vienna), well ahead of the odds.

Because of its size, the Denver airport commission helped the firm in another important way. It provided the economic base for producing outstanding entries in design competitions. While the airport work was in the office, the firm was able to win competitions for a state laboratory and office building in Olympia, Washington (1989), the National Cowboy Hall of Fame in Oklahoma City (1992), and for the Clark County Government Center in Las Vegas, Nevada (1992). These commissions not only gave the firm valuable stature in the area of government facilities and museums, but represented their initial reach beyond the borders of Colorado. A perceived geographic limit was breached, and the way was paved for other government office complexes.

The partners' devotion to design competitions as a way to win jobs stems in part, of course, from their good record for winning them. But even a losing competition entry has a lot of value to the firm, says Fentress. You can still impress subsequent clients with your competition design, and your design team has a unique learning opportunity in comparing solutions to a problem they have studied in depth. Design competitions are also an excellent opportunity to diversify the practice, without having to show prior experience in that building type—as with the government work cited earlier.

Yet another advantage of design competitions for a firm with high design aspirations is that clients holding competitions are typically looking for strong, unconventional concepts. The firm's staff gets a chance to conceptualize more freely. Capping all these other advantages of design competitions, says Fentress, is that they replace a lot of marketing effort. You don't need, he observes with perhaps undue modesty, a "front man" with the charm and persuasiveness that the term implies. Though American architects perennially complain that competitions cost them too much money, it's a question of spending the money on productive staff work versus a lot of marketing material, travel, and entertainment—and a lot of the principals' hours.

While Fentress may not consider himself to be a legendary "front man," he has a wealth of wisdom about how to deal with clients. He points out, for instance, that developer clients and corporate CEOs want to see only fully developed conceptual designs, which they accept or reject very quickly. With government clients—or any clients practising group decision-making—it is essential to reveal a concept in stages and get them committed at each stage, even if you've actually completed the design. Confronted with a fully developed concept that's new to them, such groups are very likely to pick it apart.

Fentress also stresses the firm's continuing interest in pursuing small commissions along with large ones, as most successful firms do. Smaller jobs provide excellent opportunities for staff moving up in the firm to take on major responsibilities. They can also be intellectually challenging and can significantly expand the firm's experience. The Ronstadt Transit Center in Tucson, Arizona, for instance—essentially an open-air bus depot—gave team members some excellent background in working with traffic engineers and community groups, and was an excellent exercise in responding to context.

The operations center

Fentress Bradburn's office says a lot about the firm. It is not in downtown Denver, but on a commercial thoroughfare about 10 minutes from the center, where the firm can have free on-site parking and a building (originally rented, now owned) with plenty of elbow room and daylight. Just inside the entrance is a spacious lobby, of showroom proportions, where a dozen or more models are exhibited. Up a sweeping stairway is a smaller lobby, populated with current working models, some being worked on there, from which offices and conference rooms open. A large, high-ceilinged drafting room on this floor has continuous windows on three sides and generous workspaces, with displays of photos and renderings on partitions and above windows. In the third-floor penthouse is a large, tall gathering space with many potential uses. On a recent day, for instance, it accommodated some 30 representatives of a client organization participating in a conceptualizing session with some of the firm's staff.

There is hardly a hint of luxury—except for the enviable amounts of light and space—little effort to add architectural chic to what started as a rental building. It's just a busy, though not frenzied, working place chosen on pragmatic grounds and adapted in an ad hoc way to the firm's needs. It is a laboratory for the creation of innovative architecture, not a monument to the architects' prestige. While Fentress Bradburn's objectives and accomplishments may be East Coast in many ways, its habitat and its working atmosphere are very Colorado. The firm is clearly in Denver, but addressing itself to the world.

John Morris Dixon, FAIA, is a writer and editor in Old Greenwich, CT, and was editor-in-chief of Progressive Architecture *magazine 1972–95.*

5   Client meeting on plans for corporate campus

Recent Works

Seoul Inchon International Airport Passenger Terminal

Design/Completion 1993/2001
Inchon Island, outside Seoul, Republic of South Korea
Korea Airport Construction Authority
Airport
Firm's role: design architect
5,935,000 square feet/551,362 square meters
46 gates, 35 million passengers annually
Precast concrete exterior wall panels, exterior granite columns, painted tubular structural steel for trusses, green insulated glass, aluminum exterior panels, point-fixed glazing system, single-ply membrane roofing, stainless steel ticket counters, granite, wood
Region: Korea
Context: Land-bridge between two islands

Seoul Inchon International Airport is located on a human-made land-bridge between two islands in the Yellow Sea, 50 kilometers west of the city center of Seoul, South Korea. Almost 6 million square feet in size, and built at a cost of $1.1 billion, the terminal is organized around a Great Hall, which contains airport operations, transportation systems, and customer service amenities. At opening in early 2001, the airport will have 46 connected, wide-body gates. With the addition of four satellite concourses at full build-out, the airport will boast 174 gates and will accommodate 100 million air passengers a year. Situated within three-and-one-half hours flying time of 40 cities with populations over one million, Seoul Inchon finds itself in an excellent position to serve as a regional hub.

In association with Korean Architects Collaborative International (KACI), Fentress Bradburn Architects was awarded the commission to design the passenger terminal by unanimous decision in an international design competition whose field included Aeroports de Paris; Helmuth, Obata & Kassabaum (HOK); Skidmore, Owings & Merrill (SOM); Leo A. Daly; Louis Berger International; and DMJM.

Rejecting the cold, homogenized, high-tech feel common to so many modern airports, the architects sought to affirm a feeling of warmth and welcome. By infusing the airport with the rich heritage of Korean culture, the design finds both overt and subtle ways to make Seoul Inchon a memorable gateway to the region, as well as a haven for weary travelers.

The passenger terminal itself is configured in a welcoming arc that embraces the traveler. The masts and catenary support system of the roof emulate the large anchored ships that sit in nearby Inchon Harbor. The gentle roof arc of ancient Korean temples is seen in the terminal's sweeping rooflines, and its exterior juxtaposes traditional images of earth and sky: dragon imagery, both large and small, distinguishes the airside of the terminal from the landside, which is symbolized by the tiger.

Structural system colonnades bring a rhythm and pattern to the space reminiscent of palace columns that pay homage to the harmony between heaven and earth. Floor patterns subtly cue passengers in navigating the airport, just as the lines of ancient Korean structures helped to direct royal processions. Daylight, which floods the space by way of extensive skylights, nurtures traditional Korean gardens indoors. Open floors in the lower level of the main terminal allow natural light to reach even the train platform level of the complex.

Travelers' comfort and convenience is addressed by way of "people movers," which ensure that passengers will walk no distance greater than 400 feet without assistance, as well as by warm colors inside the terminal, user-friendly spatial layouts, easy-to-access retail spaces, and high-tech amenities.

"...we [the architects] would have our discussions and critiques, that we didn't want this building to be like a building in Chicago, New York, Los Angeles, Paris, or some other place. We wanted it to feel like it was Korean, and to be of Korea. You can see that in the design of the building as we carried it through. As I got the opportunity to view the other nine competitors, you could place each of those entries in another city around the world."

Curt Fentress, *Competitions Magazine*, Fall 1995

1 Overall view
2 Night view, terminal at left, concourse stretching to right

Opposite:
    Glass curtainwall slopes outward over jetway.
4 Jetways protrude from rounded end of concourse.

5 Section of concourse
6 Section of main terminal, including Great Hall at left
7 Roof masts reference ships in nearby Inchon Harbor
8 Jetway curtainwall reflects image of concourse

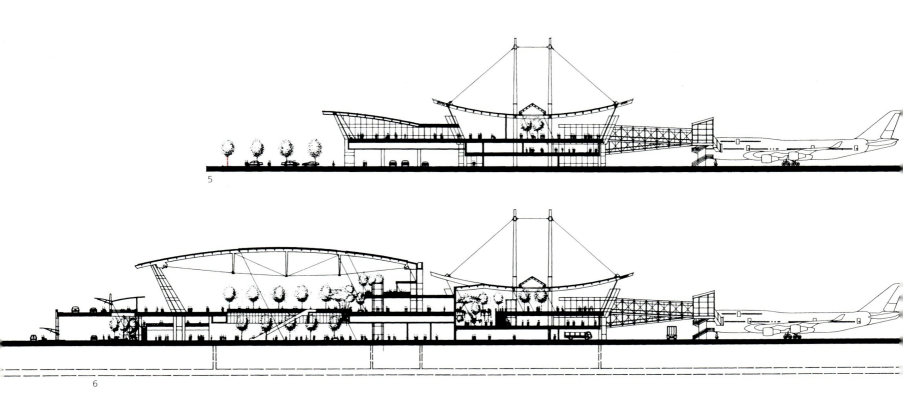

9

9　Glass curtainwall is held in place by cable-truss system.
10　Curbside shading devices evoke Asian building motifs.

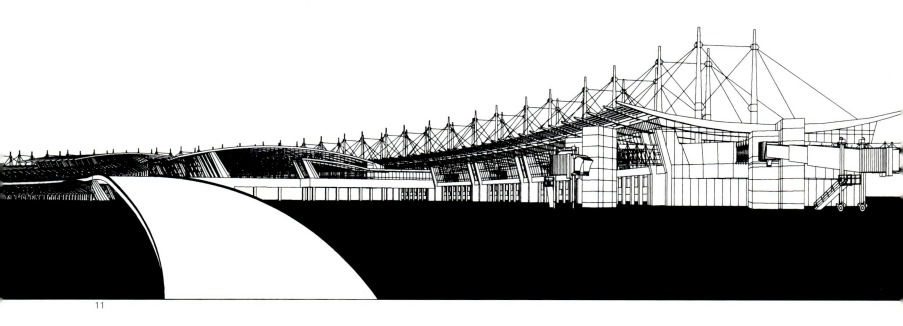

11

12

13

11 Line drawing of main terminal
12 Granite frames two-story jetway entrance into concourse.
13 Masts atop roof flank skylights over concourse.
Opposite:
    Shading device curves with the curbside arc.

16

17

Opposite:
   Wave-form lamps contrast with the curtainwall grid.
16 Coniferous trees tower inside expansive Great Hall.
17 Shape of wave-form lamps resonates with trees.

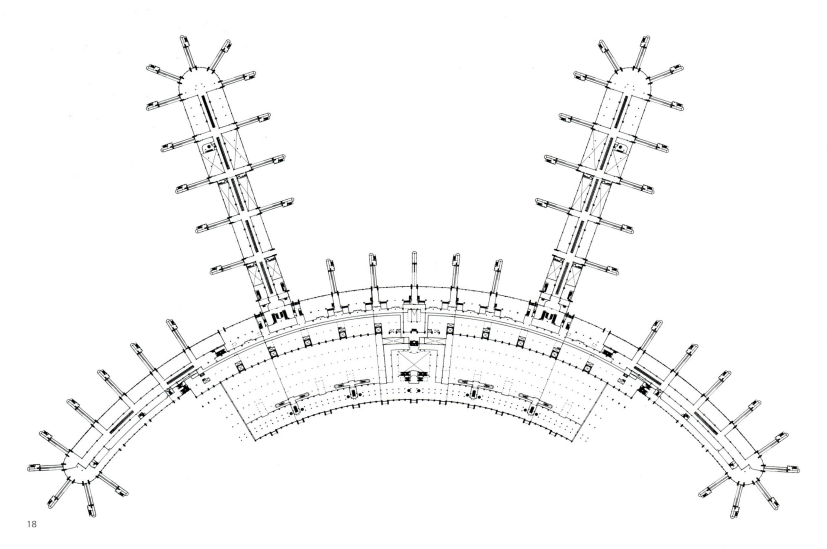

18 Floor plan of passenger terminal
19 Information desk near sloping glass curtainwall
Opposite:
    Skylights in Great Hall flood the interior with light.

21

22

23

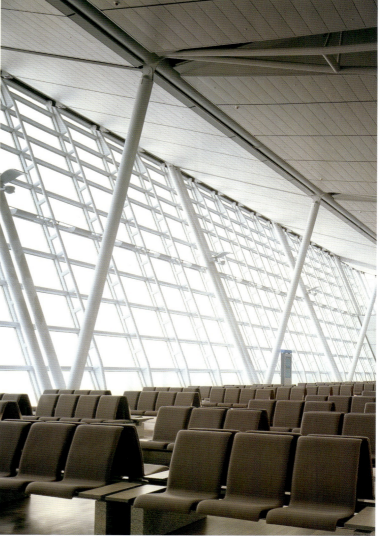
24

25

21 Columns and lintel frame departure gate.
22 Skylights allow for cultivation of interior gardens.
23 Concourse at night
24 Glass curtainwall slopes at waiting area.
25 Baggage claim area

Regional Transportation Commission and Regional Flood Control District Headquarters

Design/Completion 1995/1999
Las Vegas, Nevada
Regional Transportation Commission and Regional Flood Control District
Civic office building
Firm's role: design architect
70,000 square feet/6,503 square meters
Sandstone, glass
Region: desert
Context: Las Vegas
Guiding metaphor: canyon walls and desert wash

1

2

A sister structure to the Clark County Government Center, the Regional Transportation Commission and Regional Flood Control District Headquarters (RTC/RFCD) recapitulates Clark County's desert imagery with undulating "canyon" walls and a stone exterior. The curvilinear walls slope outward from the base of the building in an asymmetrical order, to replicate the complex nature of a canyon and to offer a similar spatial experience.

The shape of the structure differs widely from the government center, which is a much more public and therefore much more open building. Only a fifth the size, the RTC/RFCD takes the form of a box canyon, an intimate space that quickly surrounds the visitor in a desert courtyard. The main building entry is from the south side, with the high "canyon" walls shading and sheltering the courtyard for most of the day. At the center of the courtyard is a low fountain of water cascading over sandstone rock.

Covered pedestrian arcades along the southern and eastern façades protect visitors from the harsh desert sun. Native plants, stone mulches and boulders form a desert setting. Canyon imagery is again evoked with vegetation rooted in stone crevices.

Goals of energy and water conservation are met with maximum use of natural light within the building by way of low-energy supplementary lighting, plus low-E glass to control solar gain and radiant heat transfer, and rows of trees on the western face of the building shade it from afternoon sun.

The RTC/RFCD, the second building to be built on the 38-acre Clark County campus, is designed using a structural bay size coordinated with the modular system furniture used by the majority of the tenants. While the prominent façades are curved, most of the building perimeter is created using straight walls based on standard grid spacings.

1   Aerial view of RTC/RFCD and Clark County Government Center
2   Aerial view of RTC/RFCD
3   South façade
4   Courtyard with sheltered water feature

Regional Transportation Commission and Regional Flood Control District Headquarters

 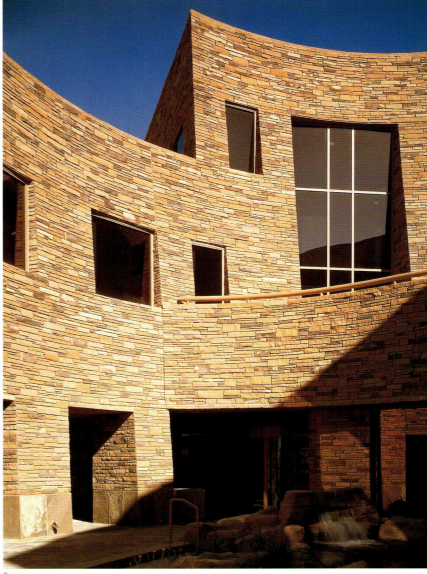

5 West façade at right, government center at back
6 Walls curve vertically and horizontally.
Opposite:
　Balcony provides retreat for employees.
Following pages:
　Undulating walls emulate a canyon.

9 Curving sidewalk continues texture and color of streambed that runs through courtyard.
Opposite:
Lobby is flooded with light at midday.

Kuwait Finance House Tower

Design/Completion 1999/2003
Kuwait City, Kuwait
Kuwait Finance House
Firm's role: architect
Office tower and retail shopping mall
30 stories—373,681 square feet/34,715 square meters
220,560 square feet/20,490 square meters of office space
153,121 square feet/14,225 square meters for commercial use
Below grade, structured, and surface parking for 297 vehicles
Reinforced concrete and structural steel frame, granite and glazed aluminum curtainwall exterior façade
Region: Arabian Gulf region of the Middle East
Context: financial and shopping districts in Kuwait City
Guiding metaphor: Arabian Gulf waters

Taking advantage of a recently lifted building restriction, Fentress Bradburn pushed the height of the Kuwait Finance House Tower to the new maximum of 30 stories, or 155 meters high. At the same time, the architects were careful to cultivate a sensitivity to local influences. The result was a bold vertical statement that is also unobtrusively symbolic of the region.

Early design concepts favored a more muscular, brawny shape, but the final configuration is highly refined, more supple and delicate. The imagery of water dominates here. In order to underscore the importance of a resource so precious to the region, the upward vertical curve represents the gentle swells and waves of the waters of the Arabian Gulf. In order to more closely simulate water, the shape is finished in a transparent, glazed aluminum curtainwall on the front of the building, with reflective metal panels at its back.

The curve is flanked on two sides by rectilinear forms clad in a vertically oriented combination of flamed and polished granite. These textures and colors combine to give the base of the tower a sense of mass extending upward to represent the solidity of the land that embraces the movement of water.

In addition to the tower's 27 floors of office space, the base comprises a commercial mall of over 150,000 square feet (over 14,000 square meters), as well as surface and below-grade parking for about 300 cars.

1

2

3

1 Early design concept, with bold upward thrust, asymmetry
2 Second phase balanced building's features.
3 Third phase of design began to refine its shape.
Following pages:
4 Final design's shimmering curve evokes images of water.
5 Back center façade is clad in reflective metal panels.

Colorado Convention Center Expansion

Design/Completion 2001/2004
Denver, Colorado
City and County of Denver
Convention/conference facility
1,500,000 square feet/139,350 square meters parking structure 1,000 vehicles
Region: high plains at the foot of the Rocky Mountains
Context: urban edge of downtown area

Fentress Bradburn Architects, the dark-horse contender in a competition to design Phase I of the Colorado Convention Center, won that commission in 1987 by shrewd urban analysis that fixed its location within walking distance of downtown Denver hotels. With the idea of attracting a greater volume of convention business, the city sponsored a ballot initiative in 1999 to expand the convention center, to more than double its size, to 2.5 million square feet. Voters approved the initiative and Fentress Bradburn was chosen in March 2000 to design the completion, or Phase II, of the building.

The new urban design concept calls for a complete re-design of the structure's exterior, giving the city an opportunity to create a new image for the building and enhance Denver's skyline. Fentress Bradburn's design emphasizes a large-scale identity on the thoroughfare side of the building, while maintaining appropriate urban scale on the side of the building that connects with Denver's downtown grid.

The thoroughfare façade is planned around an egg-shaped lecture hall that encapsulates a 5,000-seat auditorium on the southwestern side of the building, a fixture that is also in tune with the adjacent performing arts complex. On the urban side, the building will be stepped back at intervals in order to disguise its massing, and to emulate the storefront-scale of the surrounding urban neighborhood.

Meeting rooms will be expanded and moved from deep within the facility to the rooftop, in order to afford visitors spectacular views of the nearby Rocky Mountains. Exhibit areas will be doubled to 600,000 square feet of contiguous space that will have more than a dozen different possible configurations. The facility will also contain a 1,000-car parking garage.

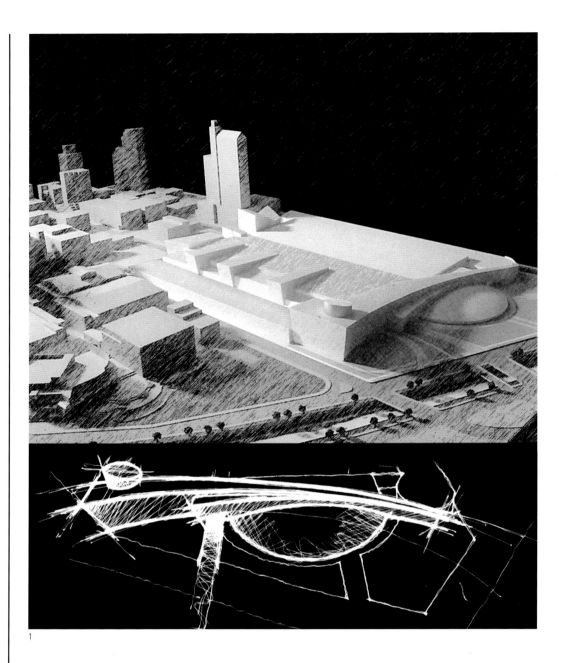

1

Other design elements include an expanded ballroom and new meeting space totaling over 80,000 square feet; a pedestrian bridge between the convention center and the performing arts complex; a rooftop restaurant; and future development potential for a 1,000-room convention hotel.

1   Computer rendering and sketch of egg-shaped auditorium
2   Existing convention facility at center

3

3   View from urban side, back toward mountains
4   New exhibit hall can be broken into 12 different configurations.
5   Lower level floor plan

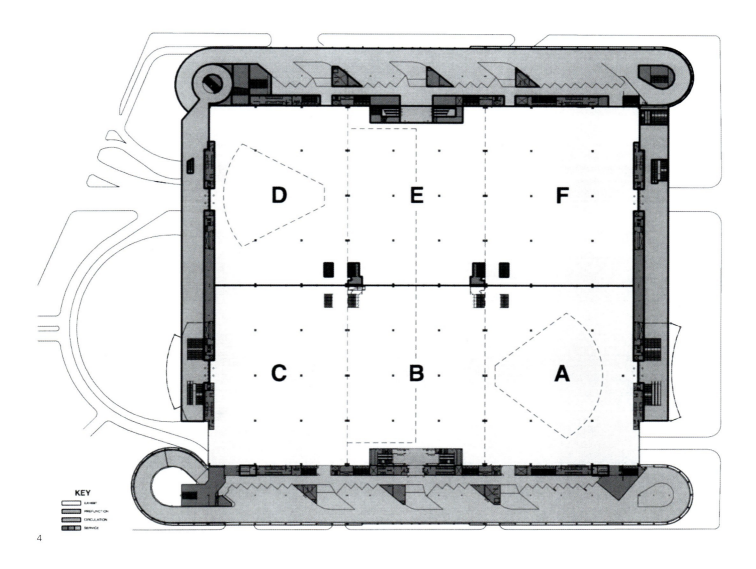

4

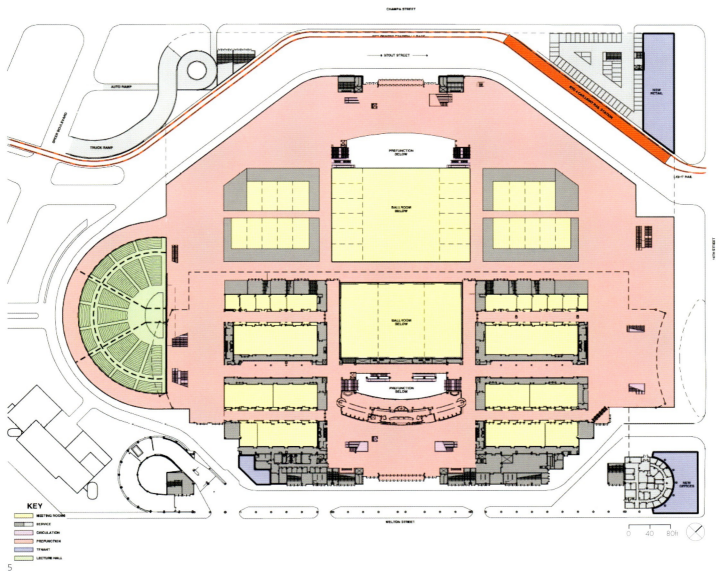

5

Colorado Convention Center Expansion 49

6　Model of existing buildings
7　Diagonal cutaway roof design concept, from urban side
8　Similar concept, from thoroughfare side
9　Egg-shaped auditorium design concept
10　Articulated arcade at left, early design concept
11　In-progress design with diagonal cutaway roof
12　Grand staircase down to 14th Street, urban side
13　Roof-top terrace will give visitors mountain views.

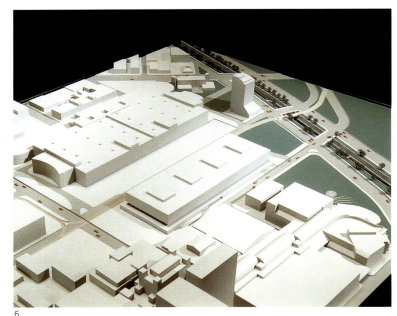

6

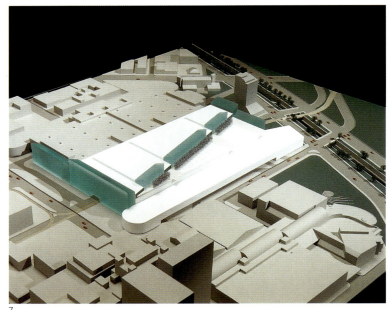

7

8

9

10

11

Colorado Convention Center Expansion 51

David E. Skaggs Federal Building (National Oceanic and Atmospheric Administration Boulder Research Laboratories)

Design/Completion 1992/1998
Boulder, Colorado
General Services Administration (GSA), U.S. federal government
Laboratories
4 stories—372,000 square feet (80,000 square feet of lab space)/34,558 square meters (7,432 square meters lab space) parking for 600 cars
Cast-in-place concrete structure, precast panels with natural stone exterior
Region: juncture of mountain and plain
Context: scientific facility

Until 1999, employees of the Boulder Research Labs of the National Oceanic and Atmospheric Administration worked in five different buildings or two campuses in Boulder, Colorado. When the General Services Administration (GSA) decided to consolidate these facilities, it was faced with creating a 372,000-square-foot structure in the midst of a predominantly residential area—in a city well-known for its social activism.

While the project did arouse community passions at the outset, ultimately Fentress Bradburn Architects found successful solutions to a vast number of concerns ranging from view obstruction and issues of scale, to energy conservation and specialized research requirements.

The building houses 698 offices, 20 conference rooms, 98 laboratories, and three major computer centers. Laboratories and automated data-processing spaces are generally located in the inner areas of the building, while office spaces—with operable windows—sit on the perimeter, affording occupants spectacular views of mountains and plains. Daylight is brought deeper into the building by way of sidelight and transom windows between the offices and the circulation corridors.

Immediate neighbors objected to the facility's size, not only because of the discrepancy in scale between the proposed structure and nearby residences, but because for many of them a building that large would almost certainly block views of the Flatiron Mountains, the scenic backdrop to the city of Boulder.

In response to publicly expressed concerns, the building is sited 900 feet from the nearest main traffic artery and 400 feet from the nearest residence. The design minimizes the building's mass first by breaking it into four blocks, each with its own configuration and orientation. These were clad partly in native stone from a nearby quarry, a feature designed to break down the scale of the building with the interplay between two different finishes. The juxtaposition of the natural stone exterior and the glass-and-metal stair enclosures at the juncture of the building sections is symbolic of the placement of a sophisticated research facility at the foothills of the Rocky Mountains. Functionally, these junctures serve as informal gathering spots for the researchers, while at the same time affording them spectacular views of the surrounding countryside. The architects sank the grade by an entire floor to create a garden level, lowering the overall height of the building to address the problem of interrupted views.

A diverse array of advanced and innovative building systems helped the building actually exceed government energy conservation standards. Collaboration with local energy provider Public Service Company resulted in the incorporation of numerous energy-efficient upgrades that are expected to reap savings for the building of more than $160,000 a year. Among these are motion sensors that turn on or off lights and localized HVAC equipment; fan coil boxes and thermostats in every office to provide room-specific control; and photocells to adjust lighting in perimeter offices, based on ambient light levels.

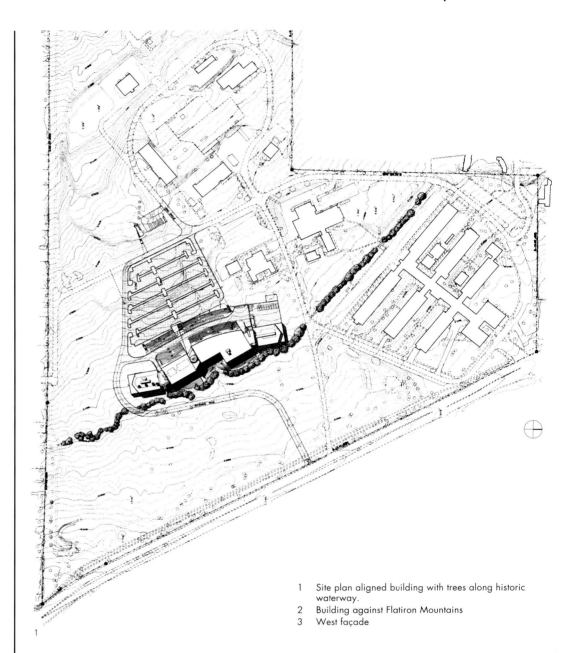

1 Site plan aligned building with trees along historic waterway.
2 Building against Flatiron Mountains
3 West façade

2

3

David E. Skaggs Federal Building

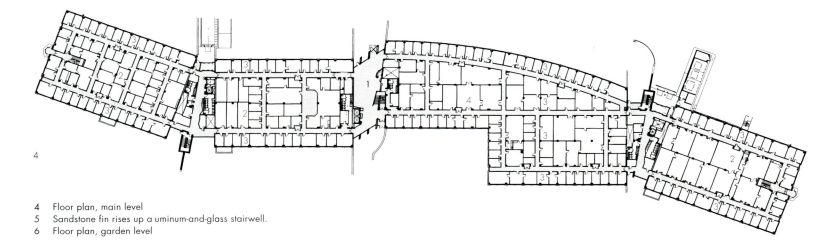

4 Floor plan, main level
5 Sandstone fin rises up a uminum-and-glass stairwell.
6 Floor plan, garden level

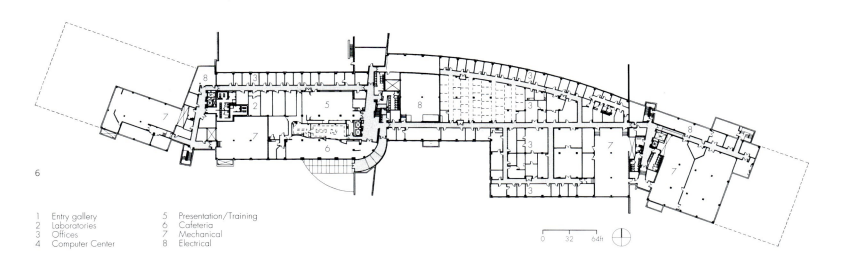

1 Entry gallery
2 Laboratories
3 Offices
4 Computer Center
5 Presentation/Training
6 Cafeteria
7 Mechanical
8 Electrical

David E. Skaggs Federal Building

7 Entrance. Sandstone bridge leads to aluminum-and-glass lobby.
8 Sleek aluminum columns mark the building's entrance.
9 Sandstone fin climbs aluminum-and-glass stairwell.
10 Wall detail, showing inset panels
11 Stone exterior links building to Flatiron Mountains.

7

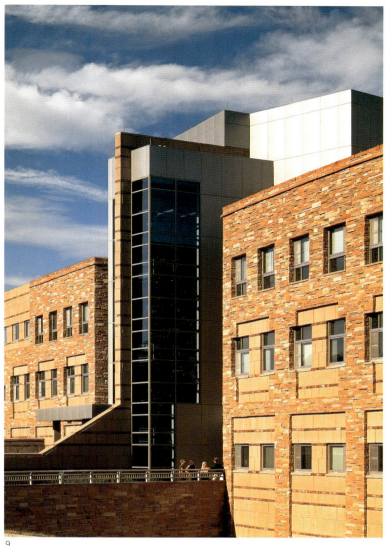
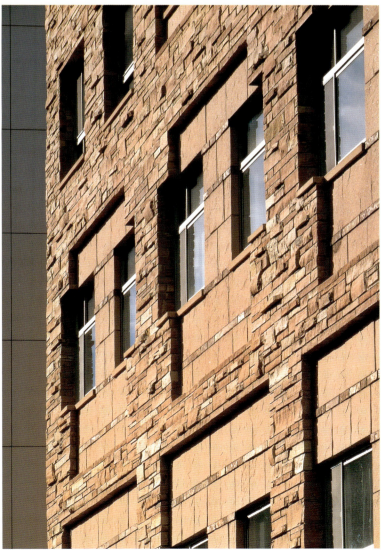
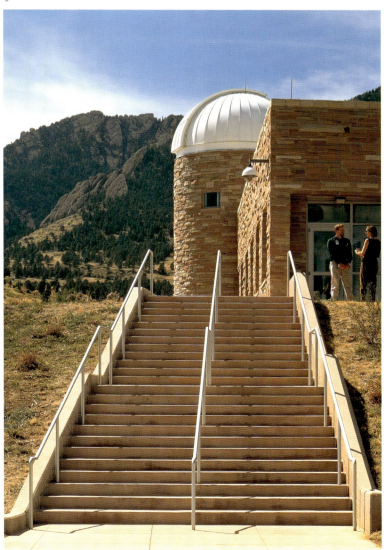

David E. Skaggs Federal Building 57

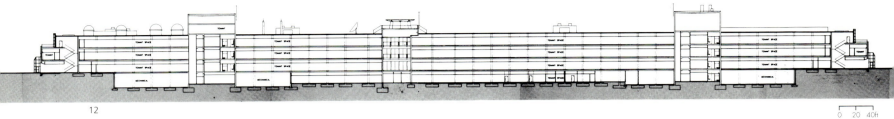

12

13

12　East elevation
13　East entrance
14　Sandstone bridge at east entrance

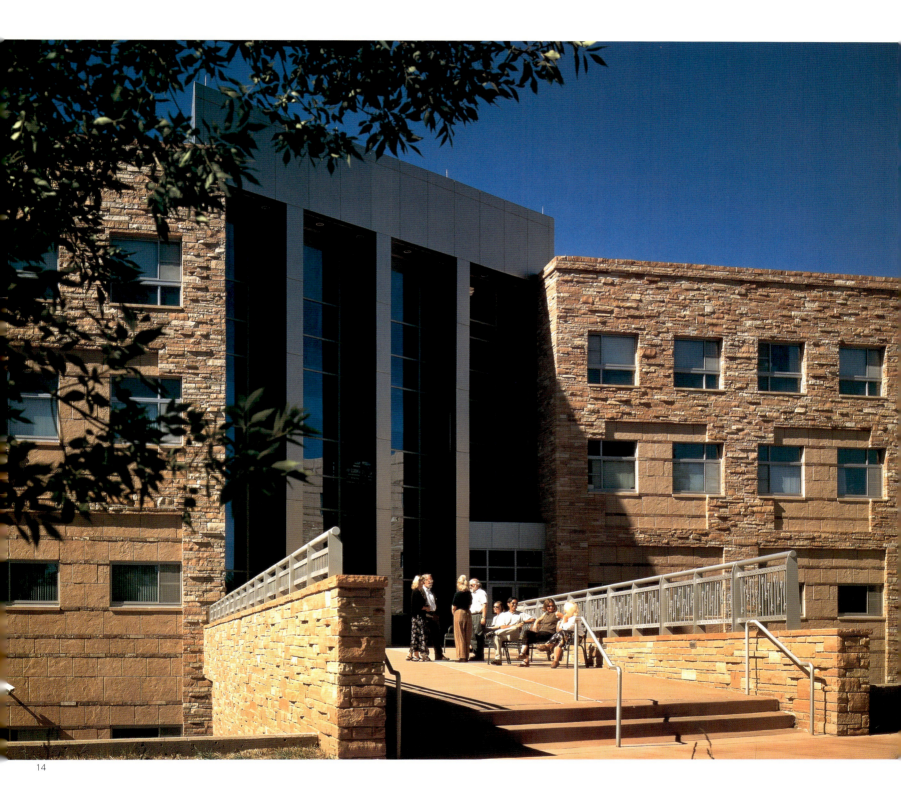

14

15 Cafeteria. Bar stools along raised counter seat singles.
Opposite:
Lobby, with spherical kinetic sculpture at bottom, satellite baffle near ceiling.

Seattle-Tacoma International Airport Central Terminal Expansion

Design/Completion 2000/2004
Seattle, Washington
Port of Seattle
Airport
240,000 square feet/22,296 square meters
21 gates, 4.8 million air passengers
Glass, steel, granite, wood
Region: Northwest United States
Context: juncture of mountains, ocean and forests

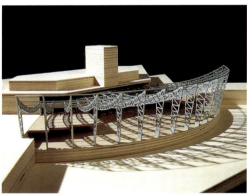

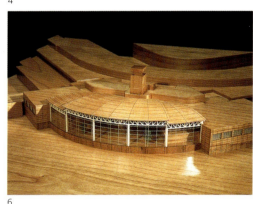

In the Northwest region of the United States, where the Washington State cities of Seattle and Tacoma lie, mountains, forests, and ocean come together in a dramatic way that is most often captured in pictures of Mount Rainier. Air travelers have been denied the pleasure of these views by an airport terminal that for many years has shut in passengers. But with the expansion of the Central Terminal at the Seattle-Tacoma International Airport, all that will change.

The Central Terminal, built in 1949, originally had observation decks from which visitors could watch landings and take-offs. Once renovations were made and restrictions were tightened because of security considerations, the terminal lost that capacity.

Chosen from a field of internationally renowned architects, Fentress Bradburn was commissioned to design the 250,000-square-foot expansion of the 50-year-old terminal. Centerpiece of the project is a 350-foot-long glass wall that stands 60 feet high. This wall creates a transparent expanse that will afford visitors spectacular views of the airfield, all the way to the Olympic Mountains.

The glass itself is curved in two directions, both vertically and horizontally, and is engineered for support by Advanced Structures Incorporated This transparent vertical plane offers contact with the outdoors that will showcase the region and invest Sea-Tac, as it is known informally, with the qualities of a true gateway. The glass wall wraps around a newly created civic space that will feature concessions, art, and interactive educational experiences in an area patterned after Seattle's famed Pike Street Market.

Behind the aesthetics are major upgrades that will increase the airport's capacity and enhance service to passengers. These include features ranging from self check-in podiums and Internet connections for laptop computers, to extensive retail and restaurants that specialize in the cuisine of the Northwest region. Other features include baggage make-up facilities, ramp level infrastructure, and a concessions distribution center.

One unusually challenging aspect of the project is its phasing. The Central Terminal Expansion is located at the intersection of four concourses, adjacent to the aircraft parking area operated by Horizon Airlines, the airport's busiest airline. The project involves maintaining seamless airport operations during relocation of airfield utilities, excavation of a basement, alternation of baggage-tug routes through the construction area, relocation and consolidation of security checkpoints, and modifications of the terminal from the curbside inward.

1 Central terminal at the time of its opening in 1949
2 Design progression: tensile-membrane roof
3 Articulated steel supports for sweeping roof
4 Rectilinear shape with clerestories
5 Glass box with rounded elements
6 Segmented glass curtainwall
7 Final design: curved glass curtainwall
8 Model showing interior with concessions and restaurants

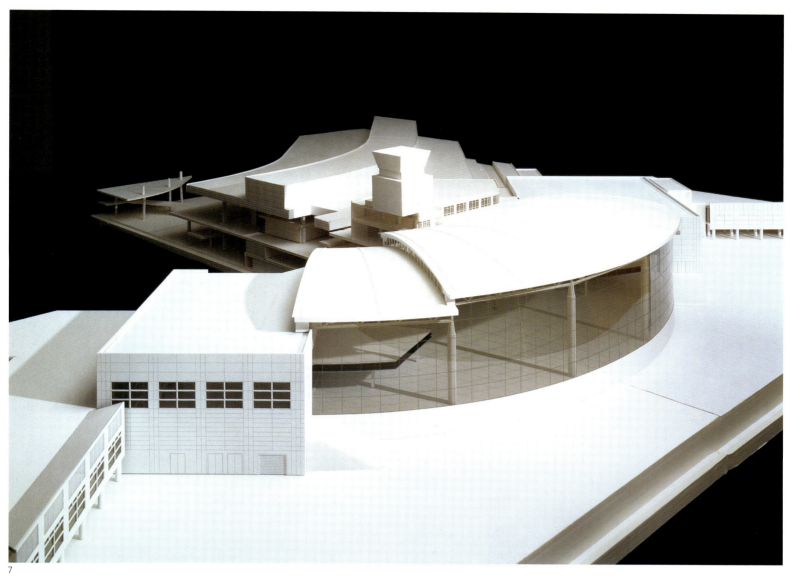

7

8

Seattle-Tacoma International Airport Central Terminal Expansion 63

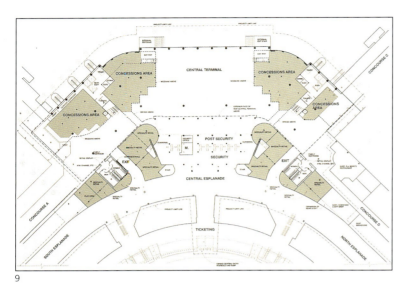
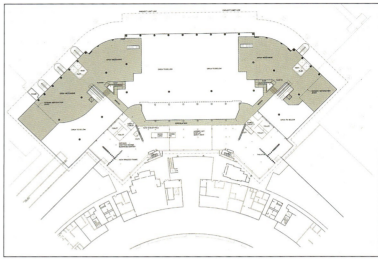

9 Floor plan, first floor, preliminary concept
10 Floor plan, second floor
11 Model, view of newly expanded terminal from tarmac
12 Glass curtainwall is curved both vertically and horizontally.

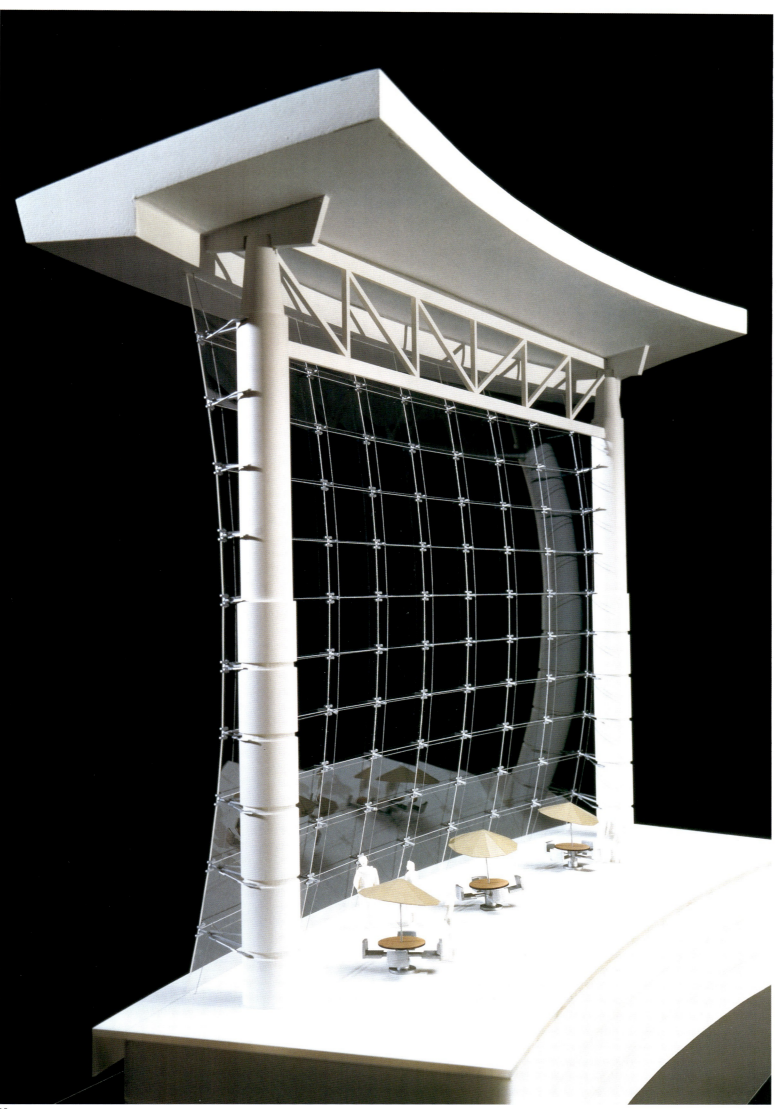

13 Model, interior of central terminal
14 Model, restaurant area
15 Model, concession area
16 Model, Pacific Marketplace
17 Abundant light fosters the use of foliage inside terminal.
18 Intimate seating areas are scattered throughout expansion.
19 Rendering hints ot mountain views through glass.
20 Rendering, lower floor of expansion
21 Rendering, from upper tier of newly expanded terminal

13

14

15

16

17

18

19

20

21

Seattle-Tacoma International Airport Central Terminal Expansion

Loveland Police and Courts Building

Design/Completion 2000/2001
Loveland, Colorado
City of Loveland
31 acres (site), 98,000 square feet/9,104 square meters (building)
Brick, concrete, architectural precast, glass pyramid skylight

The design for the Loveland Police and Courts Building uses a variety of shapes and textures to provide a welcoming but dignified presence for this city building. A simple pyramid shape at the entrance communicates the structure's civic function while clearly identifying the entrance for visitors. A colored concrete masonry base grounds the structure, in reference to historic buildings in the area. A thin white layer tops the base, shifting levels in rhythm with the window openings. The variegated colors of the brick masonry give the building an organic texture in contrast to the trim, rectilinear lines of the structure. On the two shallow wings of the building, this texture is cut by straight lines of dark brick at regular intervals. On the rounded 'drum' form at the center of the building, a diamond-shaped grid is superimposed over this pattern. This and the pyramid over the circular atrium contrast the building's curvilinear aspects with its inherent angularity—a tension that energizes and unifies the building. The dome roof is clad in metal, in stark contrast to the texture of the brick masonry. Light-colored architectural precast concrete copings at the top of the building help reduce the massing of the structure.

Within the courts facilities, three separate circulation paths are provided (public, private and secured) maximizing building safety and ease of use for all court participants. Six city and county agencies are to be consolidated within the building, including the police department, city attorney and municipal courts, as well as county courts, probation department and district attorney. The site plan allows for a large passenger drop-off area and ample landscaping.

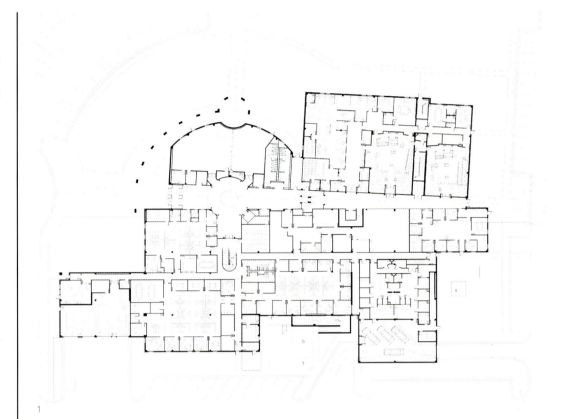

1

2

1 Floor plan, main level
2 Northeast façade
3 North section
4 East section
5 West section
6 North façade

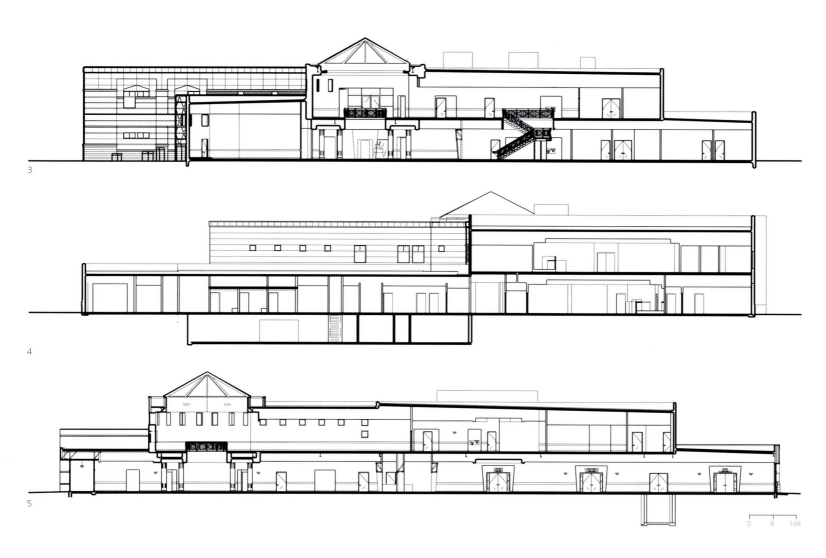

Loveland Police and Courts Building **69**

Colorado State Capitol Life-Safety Renovation

Design/Completion 2000/2005
Denver, Colorado
State of Colorado
Historic renovation
Iron, masonry, concrete and marble

The Colorado State Capitol, which is more than a century old, literally embodies the state in its use of such native materials as Fort Collins sandstone, Gunnison grey granite, ornate floors and stairs from Marble, Beulah rose onyx wainscoting, and the State's gold leaf that adorns the dome. While the building has undergone much modernization, many of these operations have had a negative impact on historic features, as well as on safety standards and functionality. The multi-year renovation of the Capitol is intended to remedy life/safety lapses.

Among the most serious conditions at the Capitol is the building's complete lack of a fire sprinkler system. A number of safety-related modifications are required to reduce the risk of potentially devastating fire and to bring the building in line with modern safety standards. Life-safety studies have also cited its non-rated floor systems, columns, and exit corridors as a danger, and have concluded that the Capitol's fire detection and alarm systems, emergency power and lighting, and exit capacity for upper floors all are inadequate.

The project's first phase covers installation of a sprinkler system within the Capitol dome and its sub-basement. Subsequent phases are planned for new work on stair extensions, dome access corridors, smoke evacuation, fire sprinklers, and fire alarm systems for the remainder of the building.

All alterations to the building are subject by law to the highest standards of respect and sensitivity for historic materials. Such high-profile additions as extended stairways and access corridors to the dome observation level must be designed carefully to blend in with the original architecture. The new sprinkler system and smoke detectors will be positioned and detailed so that they will neither detract from their surroundings nor attract unwanted attention.

1

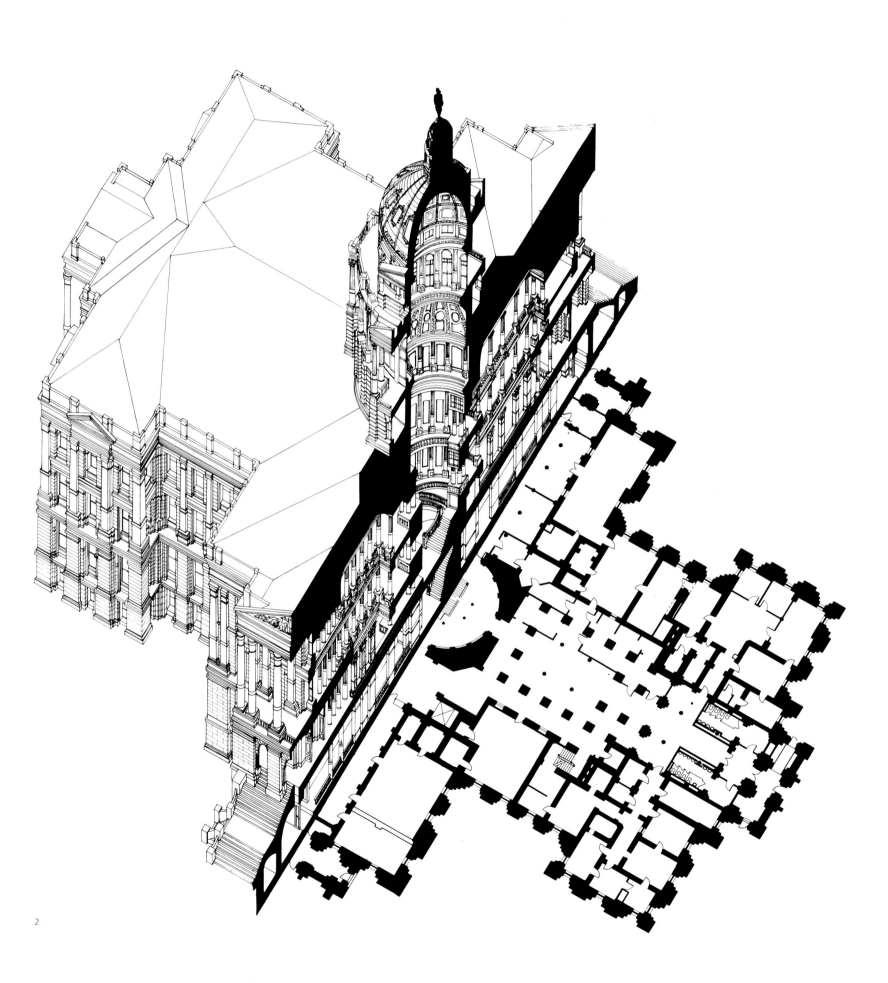

1 Original architectural drawings for State Capitol
2 Cutaway view with floor plan

Colorado State Capitol Life-Safety Renovation 71

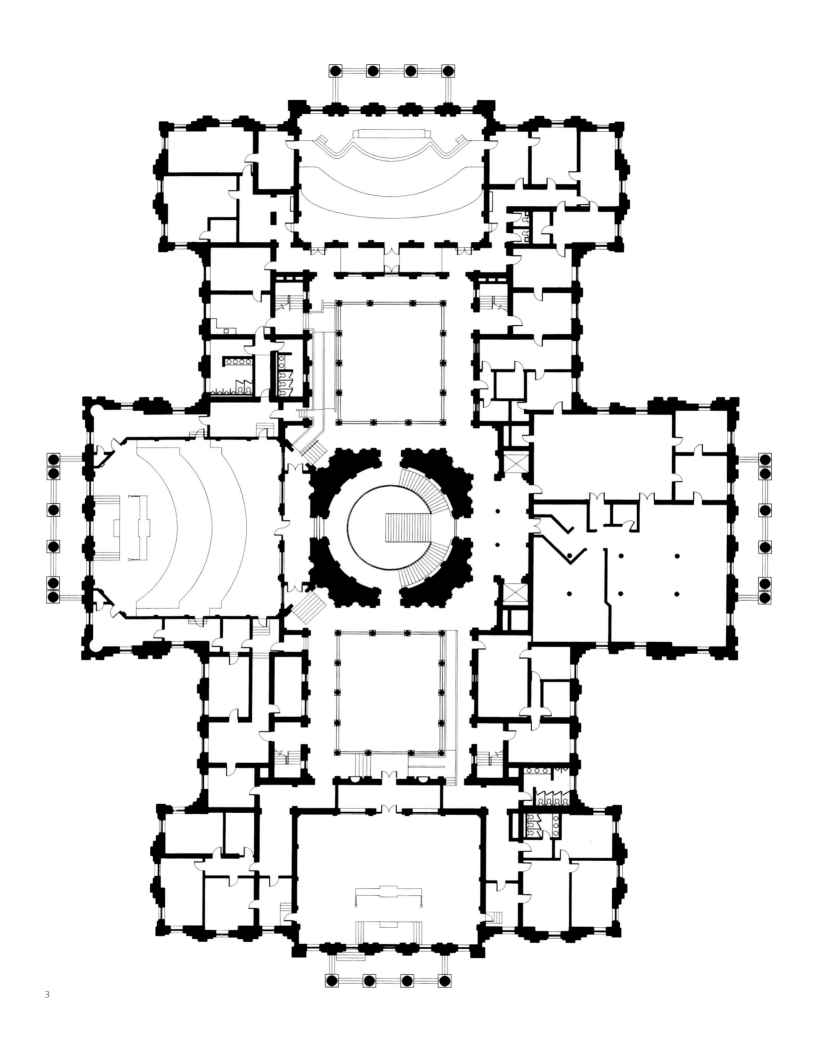

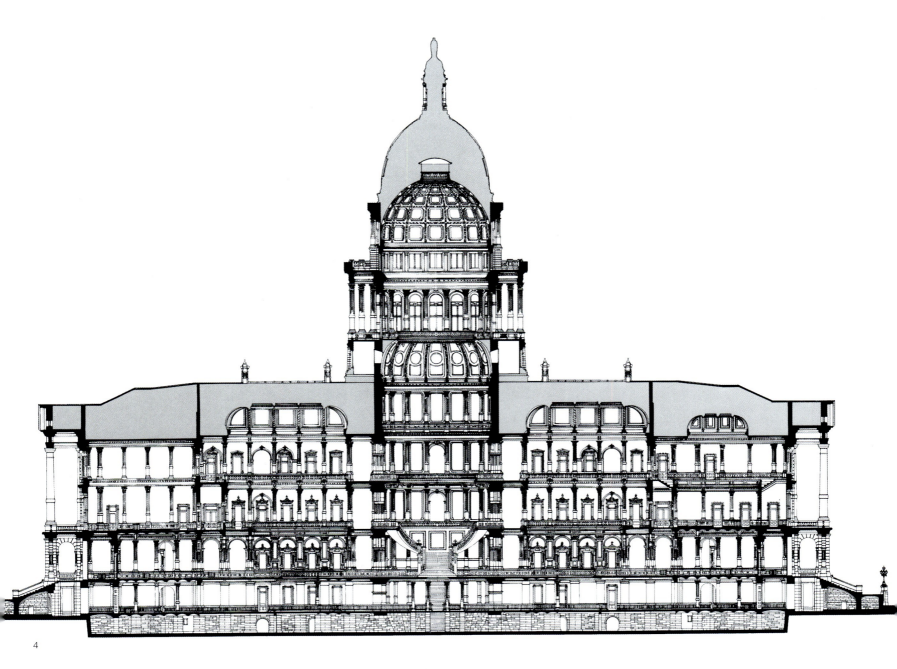

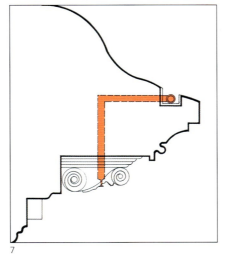

3 Floor plan
4 Section, north façade
5 Circular stairway rising to lower reaches of dome
6 Detail, top of columns, just below top-most windows
7 Detail of sprinkler piped through cornice scroll
8 Detail of scroll supports

Colorado State Capitol Life-Safety Renovation **73**

421 Broadway Renovation/Expansion

Design/Completion 2000/2001
Denver, Colorado
Fentress Bradburn Architects
Office building
10,800 square feet/1,003 square meters expansion (reception and gallery: 3,400 square feet/316 square meters, conference rooms: 3,400 square feet/316 square meters, studio space: 4,000 square feet/372 square meters)
Corrugated steel, stainless steel sheet metal, glass, Kalwall
Region: juncture of plains and mountains
Context: urban area adjacent to downtown

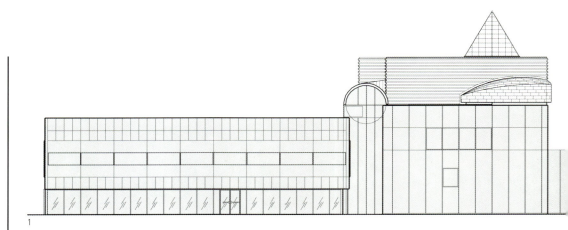

1

2

1   East elevation
2   Southeast façade
3   Open stairway, with Bronco Stadium picture on stairwell wall
4   Lit pyramid atop building at night
5   Denver skyline in the distance, with pyramid at left
6   Exterior day shot
7   Computer rendering aerial, southeast façade
8   Northern end of building, computer composite shot
9   Barcelona chairs in gallery seating area

Built for an insurance company in the late 1970s, 421 Broadway became Fentress Bradburn's office in 1992. The original building is raised on concrete pilotis, which afforded the firm extensive covered parking. The ground level featured a small glass entryway and reception area. This served the firm's needs until 1998, when it began to expand.

In 1999, Fentress Bradburn undertook a new renovation and expansion that has enlarged the 29,000-square-foot structure by almost 11,000 square feet on three different levels. The ground level of the building has been expanded to include a 3,400-square-foot gallery with an overhead lighting grid, a space that contains models of the firm's work, and accommodates traveling architectural exhibits. An open stone-and-metal stairway in an overlapping 'x' configuration leads upward out of the new gallery and reception area to a second floor working design studio that can be re-configured to address individual project design issues. This space is surrounded by the partners' offices and five conference rooms, one large enough to accommodate up to 40 people.

Leading out of this gallery area, past the curved wall decked with many of the firm's 145 design awards, is a passageway to the open design studio. This area has been expanded to add 30 more design stations to the existing 76, and to provide a new flexible, loft-like work area with expansive wall space and high ceilings—an area that can be organized for individual project charettes.

Up a stairway from the studio passageway is the firm's renovated kitchen and employee dining area, as well as the newly designed marketing department office on the firm's fifth level. A penthouse was added to the building on the seventh level, with a new 30 x 30 foot conference room. This is crowned with a translucent pyramid skylight fitting into a ceiling that has been raked back to allow the fullest possible penetration of daylight. Adjacent to this space is a small gallery and reception area near the building's centrally located elevator, and another conference room with views of the downtown Denver skyline and the nearby Rocky Mountains. The conference area is intended for design presentations and charettes. The area is accessible to a 30 x 30 foot open roof deck with views to the Rockies and downtown Denver.

Also part of the renovation and expansion is a basement workout area for employees, complete with strength and conditioning machines, showers and lockers. The space is expansive enough to accommodate aerobics and yoga classes.

3

4

5

6

7

8

9

421 Broadway Renovation/Expansion

11

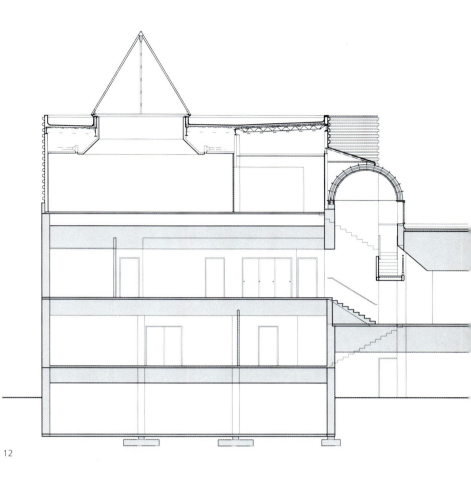

12

13

10 At night, pyramid glows atop conference level.
11 Small rooftop conference room has view to Denver skyline.
12 Section of northern end, showing top level expansion
13 Pyramid floods new conference room with light.

421 Broadway Renovation/Expansion **77**

Complex Suria Merdeka
(Kuching Town Centre)

Design/Completion 1997/2004
City of Kuching, Province of Sarawak, Malaysia
HAL Development Son. Bhd., Kuala Lumpur, Malaysia
Urban design
750,000 square feet/69,675 square meters
Phase I two 26-story office buildings, museum, retail, parking for 1,060 cars
Phase II 15-story, 80-unit residential tower, parking for 84 cars
Phase III 128-room hotel, 10,000-square-meter convention center and parking for 306 cars
Region: Malaysia
Context: urban setting

A city simultaneously embodies many different realities that give definition to its sense of place. Its public spaces must project a symbolic presence to which those realities can respond. Any new urban intervention must respect this presence, but it can also strengthen the building patterns that balance a city's living and working habits.

The Complex Suria Merdeka will be a new heart of the city for Kuching, a Malaysian urban area in the province of Sarawak. Fentress Bradburn's site plan creates this complex in harmony with the city's existing historical center. The configuration selected from an array of choices is a cross-axial composition centered around a grand outdoor "room," with substantial development at the edges of the 10-acre site.

The project will begin at the southern end of the site, with construction of two 26-story office buildings, a new museum to complement the existing off-site historical museum, parking for more than 1,000 cars, and a covered civic outdoor space bounded on the west by a low semi-circular retail structure. The project's middle phase will add a 15-story, 80-unit residential tower west of the civic room. The final phase will create a 10,000-square-meter convention center and a 128-room hotel to the north.

The outlines of the building reflect traditional flower-petal and star patterns, shapes also articulated in the roof of the public area. This structure protects the space from the elements but leaves it an open, outdoor "room." The flora that inspires these patterns is close at hand in a series of terraced gardens and fountains that cascade down a hill from the public space toward a park northeast of the site. A grand stair to the east connects the site with a pedestrian bridge leading to the historic Sarawak Museum.

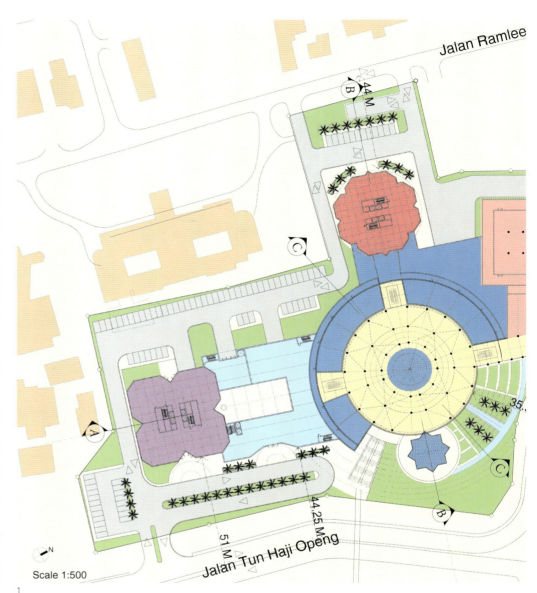

1 Master plan, showing circular civic "room"
2 Early design concept, with bridged high rises
3 Early design, with stepped residential high rises
4 Final design, with hotel/convention center at top left
5 Computer rendering of central civic space and aerial view of site

Research Complex I (University of Colorado Health Sciences Center)

Design/Completion 1999/2004
Aurora, Colorado
University of Colorado Health Sciences Center
Research laboratories
Firm's role: architect
600,000 square feet / 55,740 square meters
Steel structure, masonry, glass and aluminum curtainwall
Region: western United States
Context: bio-science research park

1 West façade from northwest; auditorium at lower left
2 Floor plans, main level

The decision to move the University of Colorado's Health Sciences Center (UCHSC) from a cramped urban location to a former United States Army medical base has become the catalyst for creation of a $5 billion biomedical research park in Aurora, Colorado. Research Complex I is one of the first components of that move—a 600,000-square-foot facility slated to open in 2004.

In building Research Complex I, UCHSC's goal is to continue to enhance its position as a nationally prominent research institution. Fentress Bradburn, working in association with Kling Lindquist of Philadelphia and GPR Planners of Purchase, New York, has designed a complex that encompasses two interconnected buildings: one 12 stories high, the other 9 stories. The two feature articulated aluminum and glass curtainwall front façades, which evoke the scientific activities within while also offering occupants panoramic views of the Rocky Mountains. The basic laboratory design is based on an open, generic module, providing enhanced flexibility for the life of the complex. The two buildings are connected by pedestrian bridges at the second, fifth and sixth levels. Similar bridges will link the structures to other buildings on the UCHSC campus. Housed within the complex will be facilities for research and medical education, including wet labs, dry labs, office space, and support space.

Acquired from the United States Department of Education following the shutdown of the former Fitzsimons Army Medical Base, the University's extensive land holdings at the site will allow for future expansion. Location was also an asset. The site is adjacent to an interstate highway exchange and is relatively close to Denver International Airport.

The University of Colorado Health Sciences Center will eventually need 1.8 million square feet of laboratory and laboratory support space in order to relocate its research campus—a move that the University is planning over a period of 10 to 12 years. At full build-out, approximately 3.5 million square feet of new and/or renovated facilities will be located at the Fitzsimons site, integrating the University's medical school with basic research and health care facilities.

At full development, the 217-acre UCHSC campus is expected to employ 18,000, and to attract $100 million annually in research funds. It will exist in tandem with a 147-acre campus of privately funded and commercial bio-science research facilities currently in design.

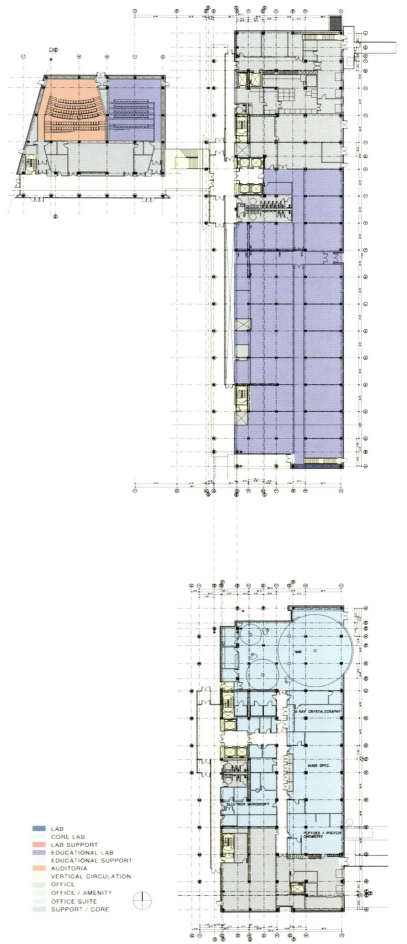

Research Complex | 81

3 East façade, showing bridges between two buildings
4 West façade, from southwest corner
5 West façade

4

5

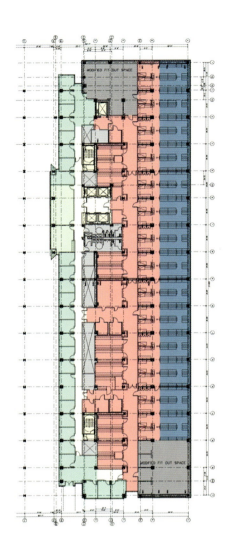

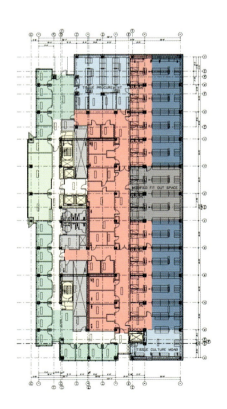

LAB
CORE LAB
LAB SUPPORT
EDUCATIONAL LAB
EDUCATIONAL SUPPORT
AUDITORIA
VERTICAL CIRCULATION
OFFICE
OFFICE / AMENITY
OFFICE SUITE
SUPPORT / CORE

6 Floor plans
7 Computer rendering, interior arcade, second level
8 Computer rendering, west façade, articulated aluminum skin
9 View from north, showing both brick and aluminum façades
10 East façade; bridges connect second, fifth and sixth levels.

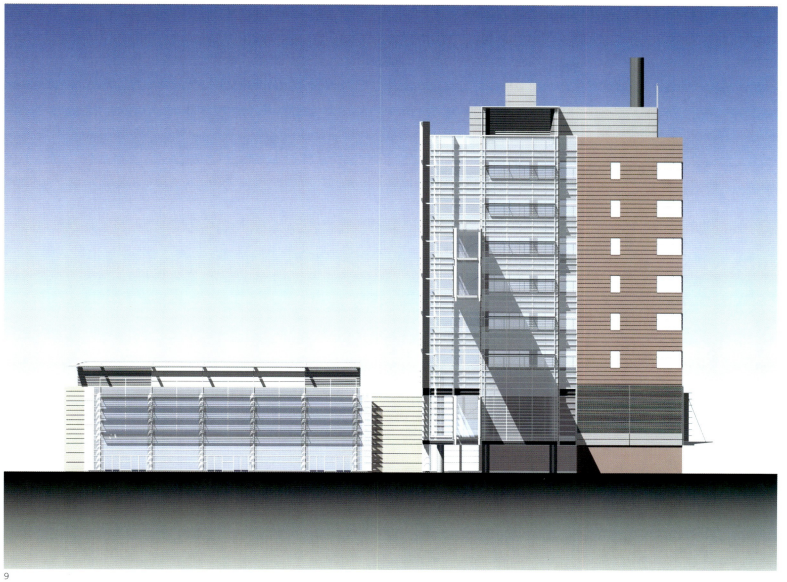
9

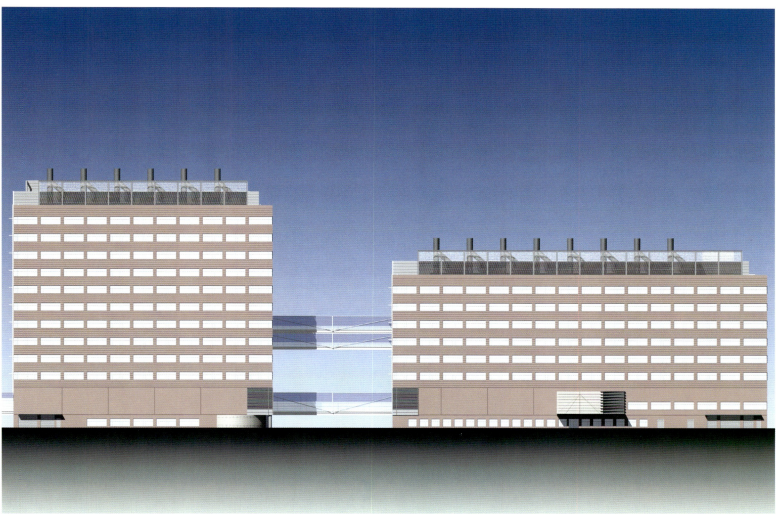
10

Research Complex I | 85

11 East façade; bridge at left connects to other structures on campus.
12 Computer rendering of plaza at auditorium

Cherry Hills Community Church Chapel

Design/Completion 2000/2002
Highlands Ranch, Colorado
Cherry Hills Community Church Chapel
36,000 square feet/3,344 square meters
Concrete, ashlar stone, wood
Region: juncture of mountain and plains
Context: foothills of the Rocky Mountains

1

The 66-acre campus of the Cherry Hills Community Church already contains buildings totalling 185,000 square feet, including a 3,500-seat main sanctuary, the church's K–8 school, office space, meeting rooms, and gymnasium. The church needed a sanctuary of more modest proportions for smaller, more intimate functions, such as weddings and memorial services, and was seeking a traditional "chapel" aesthetic, in contrast to the main sanctuary's more modern and informal appearance.

The northwestern corner of the campus, on which the new chapel is to be located, is a dramatic promontory that converges to a point at the corner of the lot, dropping down on all sides toward a major traffic intersection. Because the chapel area is the first visible sign of the church campus on approach, it could create a memorable foreground for the entire site.

Fentress Bradburn proposed using the new chapel to organize the campus with a pair of intersecting pedestrian pathways that, in plan, form a cross. One of these would run from the chapel on the northwestern end of the site, along the eastern side of the existing buildings, to a small semi-circular meditation park planned at the southern end of the campus. A low wall along this pathway would unite the new chapel with the existing campus buildings. Landscape features, such as a colonnade of cypress trees, as well as lighting along the length of this pathway, would also help to establish this axis for visitors entering the church campus. As one approaches the chapel, one would encounter a cross axis running along the chapel's front in a low-profile bar that houses the chapel's ancillary functions. These include a prayer room with its own private garden niche in the base of the bell tower.

For the building itself, the client wanted a simple shape that could be recognized at a distance as a chapel. Initial discussions dwelled on quaint images of old English country churches, with an emphasis on humble materials such as stone for the exterior and unadorned wood for floors, ceiling, and pews.

The design is a traditional peaked-roof church with a squared-off bell tower. The low wall linking the chapel to the existing sanctuary shares its ashlar-stone exterior and is punctuated at regular intervals with pointed-arch openings that echo the door and stained-glass window openings in the church proper.

Twelve-foot ceilings in the narthex, or lobby, give it a spacious feel. Inside the sanctuary, the heavy wooden ceiling soars dramatically at a 50-degree angle to a point more than 100 feet high. Under it, high stone walls are punctuated with stained-glass windows. The only asymmetrical element in the building is the prowed stone apse at the front of the church, where a narrow vertical window runs from floor to gable. This opening throws a reverent wash of light across the left side of the chancel wall, where a large cross is exhibited.

The entire floor beneath the chapel is devoted to a conference center. Because of the slope of the site, this expansive area is afforded windows, glass doors, and a paved terrace, all with spectacular mountain views.

1 Site plan, chapel at top
2 Model of site, from the southeast, chapel above right
3 Model of site, from northeast
4 Model, west façade
5 Model, from southwest
6 Model, showing floor-to-ceiling opening at front
7 Rendering. Light from front opening draws attention to cross.

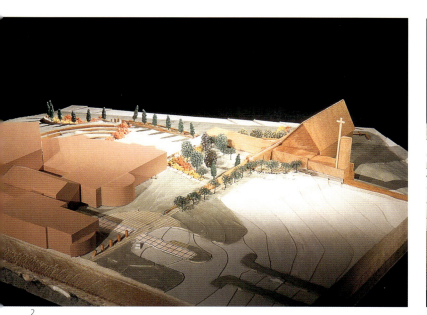

2

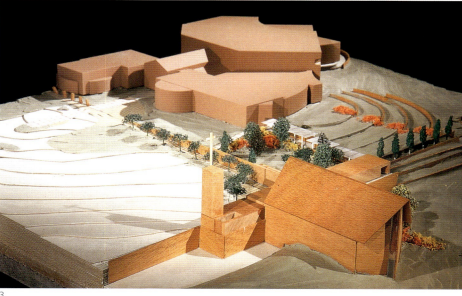

3

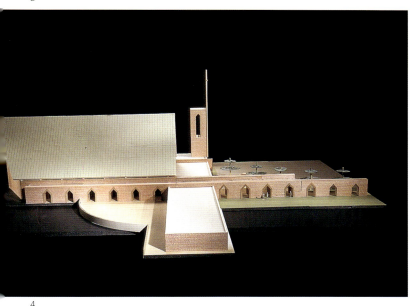

4

5

6

7

Cherry Hills Community Church Chapel

J.D. Edwards & Co. Corporate Campus

Design/Completion 1996/2003
Denver, Colorado
J.D. Edwards & Co.
General office space/campus master plan
1,200,000 square feet/111,480 square meters
(Buildings I–V)
parking structures for 4,779 cars
Steel, concrete, architectural precast, sandstone, glass
Region: western United States
Context: software development firm

The 875-acre Denver Technological Center office park already houses 35,000 employees at 1,000 companies, in almost 9 million square feet of Class A office space located in southeastern Denver and adjoining suburbs. Business-application software developer J.D. Edwards & Co. acquired a parcel of land that could be termed the flagship property of the Denver Tech Center. The J.D. Edwards site is located at the very northern end of the office park, at one of the busiest highway intersections in the State: the confluence of Interstate-25 and Interstate-225.

The project began as a commission for a single building and, because of unanticipated corporate growth, quickly blossomed into an entire corporate campus. Master planning at the beginning of the project served the client well, as a total of five buildings were eventually designed, along with a hotel and other corporate site amenities such as a cafeteria and training center.

In the design of the campus, four mid-rise structures are arrayed around a planned 22-story office tower. The tower serves as the hub of a series of radiating axes that cut lengthwise through each of the smaller structures.

In the façades of the four smaller buildings, there is a play of vertical and horizontal rectangles, not only in the ivory precast frame, but in the organization of glass panes within this frame. This orderly, rectilinear configuration serves as a subtle metaphor for the technological endeavors to which the buildings are dedicated. Sandstone and buff precast panels serve to accent the ivory grid as well as to cap it. Each building features a stately, rounded lobby in contrasting sandstone—a form that protrudes from the center of the building to mark its entrance. One building features a two-story atrium

1

which rises on the exterior of the building for several stories, mirrored at the top by a semicircular indentation. The others echo these lines with a two-story protrusion on the exterior, which is topped by large vertical rectangles that push above the cornice line. The lobby interiors feature mahogany millwork and stone flooring in an intricate pattern.

The 22-story high-rise office tower is designed with sloping outer walls, which creates a dynamic shape. Its subtle triangular motif, played out against the horizontal striation of the tower and the rising vertical planes, is fully realized in the pyramidal pinnacle and spire that crown the building.

The campus features a 20,000-square-foot data center, on-grade and below-grade connectors between buildings, and open floor plans to accommodate systems furniture and the creation of teaming communities within departments. The buildings' mechanical and electrical systems include a cable tray raceway system, dual fiber-optic feeds to each of the 29,000-square-foot floors, and an enhanced power supply. A generator farm provides backup power for the data center and other mission-critical business operations.

1 Complex emerges out of grass field.
2 Buildings are connected by shaded arcades.
3 Proposed tower will serve as hub to four mid-rise buildings.
4 Construction shot as buildings are readied for occupancy

J.D. Edwards & Co. Corporate Campus   91

5 Floor plans for all seven levels
6 Rounded lobby continues up Building III.
7 Employee cafeteria
8 Curvilinear shapes welcome visitors to reception areas.

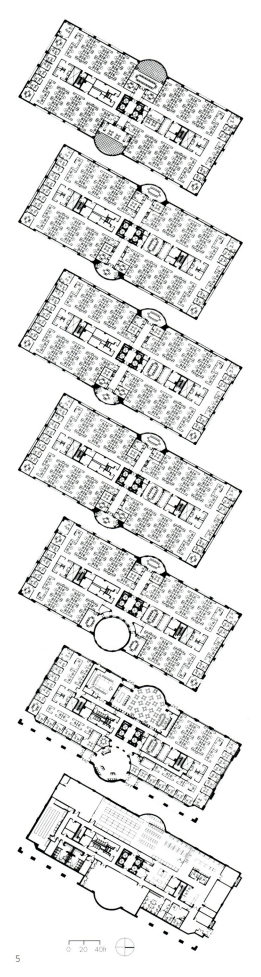

Competitions

Clark County Government Center

Design/Completion 1993/1995
Las Vegas, Nevada
Clark County (Nevada) General Services Department
Government administration buildings
Firm's role: master plan, site plan, architecture, space plan, interior design
6-story main building, three one-story buildings, 350,000 square feet/32,200 square meters
Steel frame, concrete core; exterior: sandstone, glass, painted metal; interior: granite, stucco, carpet, gypsum board
Region: southwestern United States
Context: desert
Guiding metaphor: the desert canyon

The composition of the Clark County Government Center is based on the circle—one of the most ancient of building forms. Here it serves to bind a myriad of disparate elements. The center comprises four buildings: a 6-story county administration building and three one-story buildings for the County Commissioners Chambers, a multi-purpose community facility, and a central plant. These are all organized around a public courtyard. From a distance, onlookers have a strong visual impression of the complex, one that stirs the emotions and piques one's interest through the use of monumental scale and striking architectural form.

The design competition
By unanimous decision, Fentress Bradburn Architects won the national competition to design the Clark County Government Center, competing against architect Antoine Predock of New Mexico, and architect Robert Venturi, author of *Learning from Las Vegas*.

It was clear from the start that there wasn't going to be anything generic about the design. "In a place like Las Vegas," says lead designer Curt Fentress, "even a civic building has to have a theme." The obvious choice was between the glitz of The Strip and the natural environment. But, the architects reasoned, the project was about the county, not about Las Vegas. And the county was enormous, with a startlingly diverse landscape of desert wash, canyons, cliffs, forest, mountains, and plains. There might not be a sense of tradition among people in Las Vegas, but there was a plethora of evocative images in the area's context and region.

The architects began exploring. Not far from Las Vegas, they visited Red Rock Canyon and Lone Mountain, a natural pyramid carved out by wind and water erosion. Farther afield, in Valley of Fire State Park, they happened onto a half-mile hike up to a rock formation called Mouse's Tank. There, they found a flood of imagery: orange rock canyon walls that undulated around them; stone formations enclosing "rooms" lit only by crevices; angulated shapes of rock strata pushed up on end; carved arches and pillars of stone; green pockets of vegetation; and petroglyphs thousands of years old. They began to see a natural order to life in that harsh environment.

Days later, it would be the hike and the place to which it led that stood out in all their research. Ultimately, this experience would structure their design. The task was to create a free-form architectural vocabulary, a sculptural language for creating a desert building.

1

2

3

4

5

Early versions
The design team began with plans based on the desert landscape. The first attempts culminated in courtyards and scattered buildings. These moved to more precise, angular geometries and objects on the landscape.

Slowly, the shapes grew more curvilinear, referencing the circle as ancient civic organizer. An axis began to emerge from this shape, a line that focused the entire complex, a sculptural armature in the landscape to which the designers could affix buildings. Eventually, this axis would align with the expressway exit that serves the site. The next step was to create a landmark and a sense of place.

1 Design progression: axis cutting circular arcade
2 Small pyramid atop rotunda
3 Skylight screen on rotunda roof, "canyon" at right
4 Pyramid enlarged, upper floors supported on columns
5 The glamour of the complex holds its own with The Strip.
6 Rock canyon imagery inspired the design of the building.
7 Final model

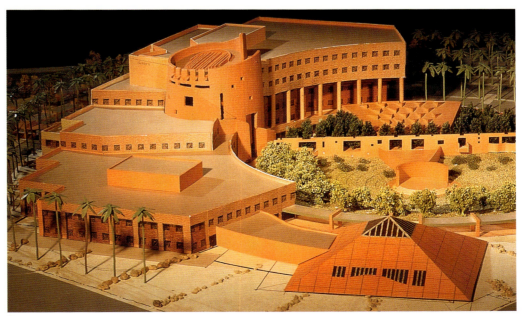

Clark County Government Center

The canyon wall

As the project developed, the design began to echo what the architects had seen in the desert. The approach to the building became the hike up to Mouse's Tank. It is flanked by pine trees. Alongside it runs a stone wall carved with petroglyphs and punctuated with openings at irregular intervals, to give people the vistas experienced in a canyon. And it is aimed directly at the rotunda that emulates Mouse's Tank.

8

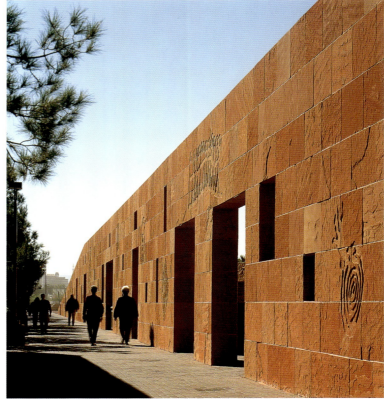

9

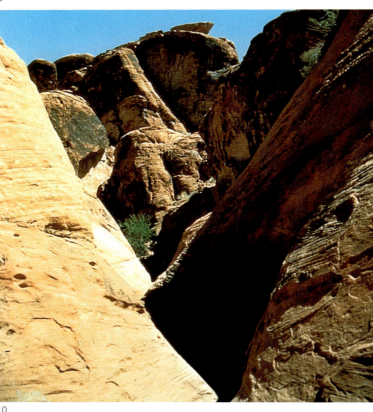

10

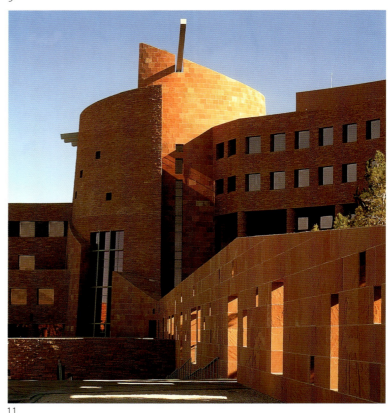

11

8   Petroglyphs on a rock wall in Valley of Fire State Park
9   Petroglyphs were carved into the approach wall.
10 Rock canyon walls, Valley of Fire State Park
11 Light penetrates openings in the approach wall.
Opposite:
    Pine allée create a sense of discovery on approach.

Mouse's Tank

"Mouse" was the name of a Paiute Native American who in the late 1800s lived in the area that is now Las Vegas. At one time, Mouse worked on a ferry that crossed the Colorado River, but he ran into trouble with settlers and became an outcast, roaming the hills and canyons of what is now Valley of Fire State Park. Mouse was able to survive in that inhospitable landscape because of a desert "tank"—a depression in the rock that catches and holds rainwater for a time after intense rainstorms. A space that is well-hidden in the maze of rock formations on the floor of Petroglyph Canyon, Mouse's Tank has become a favorite attraction for visitors to Valley of Fire.

As desert images began to play upon the minds of the designers, Mouse's Tank emerged as a symbol—a vessel of resources and a refuge—an appealing metaphor that also helped focus other imagery.

As visitors enter this space, they discover a deep, shaded room, a respite from the desert sun. The designers saw that this central rotunda was the main organizing element from which the rest of the building could grow.

13

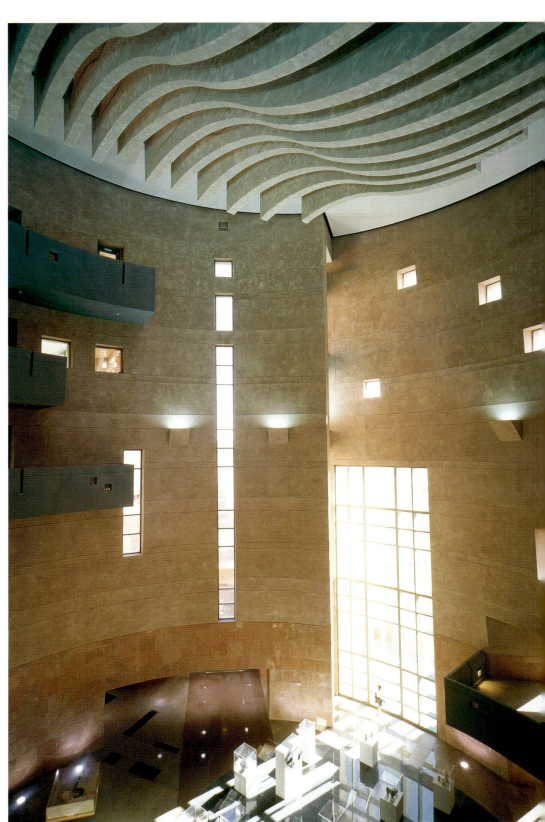

14

13 Mouse's Tank
14 Interior lobby, rotunda
15 Elevation of entire complex
16 Rotunda rises like a towering canyon wall.

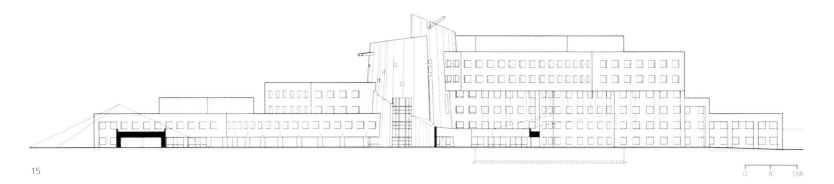

15

16

Clark County Government Center

Oasis in the desert

"At a cocktail party before the competition, I heard people say, 'We're normal. We're not all showgirls or gamblers or dealers.' They wanted an alternative to The Strip, a place with dignity and an element of solitude, as well as a sense of place, somewhere they could gather as a community of citizens. This is where the inspiration for adding an amphitheater to the facility came from. If you go there to hear a classical music concert, you'll come away with a very different impression of who lives in Las Vegas than if you simply visited the casinos."

Curt Fentress, principal in charge of design

The government center is organized around a multi-functional county courtyard and shaded pedestrian spine. The shaded circular arcade completes the curving form of the building. Aligned radially with the columns of the building are three rows of trees framing a sloped lawn amphitheater. A centered, raised platform creates the stage. The amphitheater, an acre and a half in area and 280 feet in diameter, is capable of accommodating almost any type of major public gathering, theater or ceremony. The central amphitheater represents the center of the community and public life. The placement of columns and trees creates a civic order that gives a natural outdoor setting for civic and community activities.

The courtyard contains the one irrigated zone of lawn within the county complex. Visually and physically accessible to all, the lawn bowl represents a careful, efficient and yet ultimately ceremonial and symbolic use of water.

17 Courtyard at dusk
18 Courtyard as a crowd begins to gather for a concert
19 Clerestories (right), upper windows are lit to frame concert stage.
20 Rendering of courtyard
21 People picnic on tiered lawn before concert stage.
22 Daylight shot of courtyard

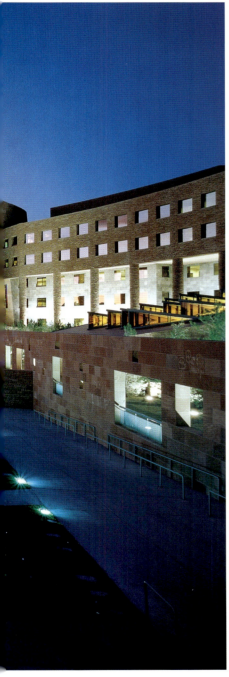

Clark County Government Center **103**

23　Ashlar stone finish contrasts with sandstone block.
24　Mouse's Tank is one of many "pothole" canyons in the region.
25　Ashlar stone emulates texture of naturally eroded pillars.
26　Geometric forms play off each other.
27　Shaded arcade curves toward rotunda.

Rock walls and pillars of stone

As the designers went back and forth from the building's requirements to the images of nature that had inspired their design, they found that it was going to work best both programmatically and aesthetically to make the higher floors larger than the lower ones. This gave them the chance to carve out underneath, just as water and wind erode canyon walls, sometimes leaving behind stone "pillars." A mix of ashlar-stone cladding with sandstone block on indented planes emulates the textures of rock faces eroded by wind and water.

The "bowl" of the building—the enfolding shape—emulates the sinuous curve of the desert wash. It is also a welcoming form, symbolic of open and accessible government. As the walls of a canyon rise up, they encircle the visitor, creating the sense of being in a room. This canyon "room" is to the desert what the town square is to the city: a ceremonial space to gather, to take refuge. The government center acts as the backdrop and support to the community, as canyon walls act as a backdrop and form-giver in the desert.

23

24

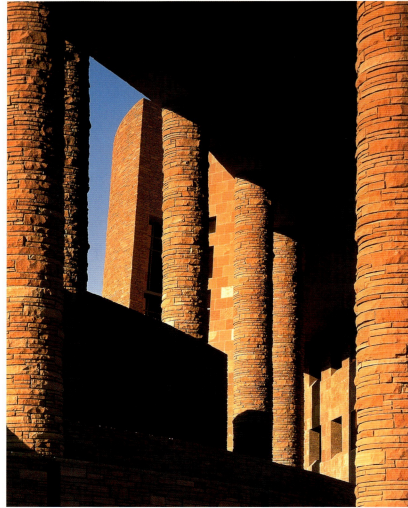

25

26

27

Clark County Government Center **105**

The mountain

Lone Mountain, a modest pyramidal formation visible from Las Vegas, became the inspiration for the shape of the cafeteria. Lower windows are slotted in a curvilinear shape that works in contrast with the angularity of the building form. The peak of Clark County's pyramid is slotted with tinted windows, which, combined with torchiere lighting on the interior, give users an exhilarating sense of sky from within.

28

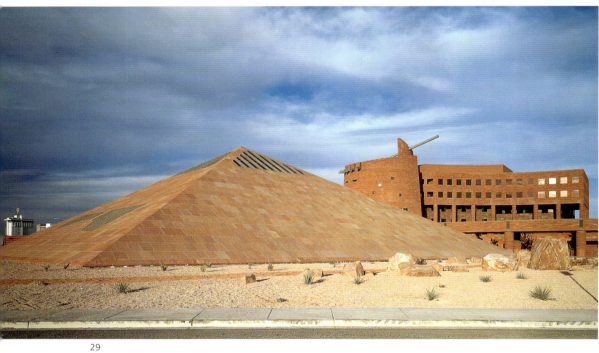
29

30

31

28 Lone Mountain, near Las Vegas
29 Pyramid with slotted windows in curvilinear shape
30 Night view of pyramid, lit from within
31 Skylights give interior pyramid exhilarating feel.

32 Prickly pear cactus
33 Pointed motif continues in inlaid wood shapes.
34 Clerestories create pointed motif in ceiling.
Opposite:
    Clerestories on roof convey sharp desert shapes.

The prickly pear cactus

The sharp edges of desert cacti provide the imagery for the design of the Commissioners' Chamber, both inside and out. The roof of the space is an intricate network of clerestory lights reminiscent of the prickly pear cactus spine system, a configuration conveying the sharp edges that mark much of desert life. The imagery is continued inside, with the pointed recesses created by these clerestories, shapes that radiate across the ceiling of that space.

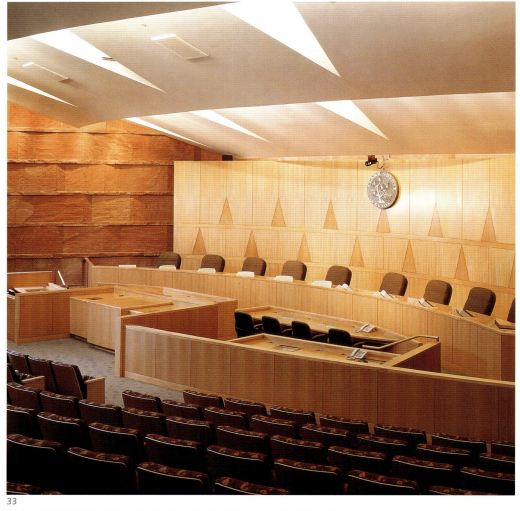

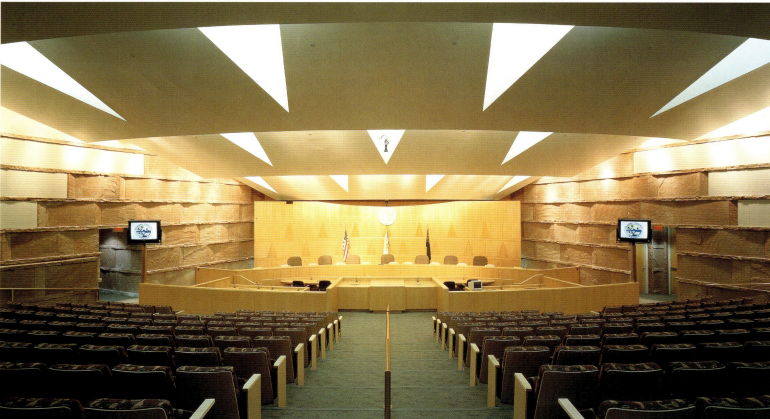

36 Floor plan, entire complex, main level
37 Light penetrating through a crevice, Valley of Fire State Park
38 Erosion-sculpted shapes inspired designers.
39 Six-story rotunda is topped by skylight and screen.
40 A triangular stairway cuts into the rotunda.
41 Torchiere lamps are modeled on desert flowers.
42 Lit coffered ceiling is reflected in circular shape on floor.
43 Floor of rotunda

Shelter from the sun

Within the lobby of the complex, the architectural vocabulary speaks in specifics. Blue granite on the floor of the lobby signifies water, a precious resource in the desert. The dark green balconies represent the startling pockets of vegetation found in canyon areas. The small openings that punctuate the walls, as well as the sculpted grid that shades the rotunda's skylight, emulate the crevices found in rock walls. Even the torchiere lamps that light the lobby were crafted to emulate desert flowers and the tough, cord-like vines that twine among these rare blooms.

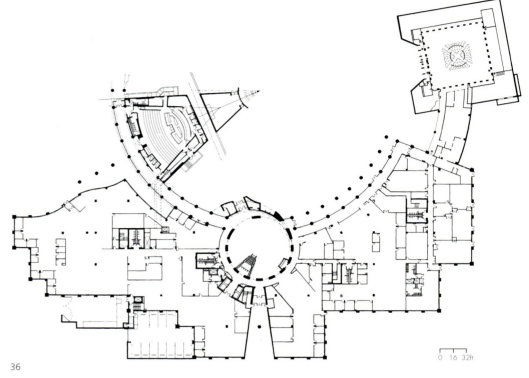

36

37

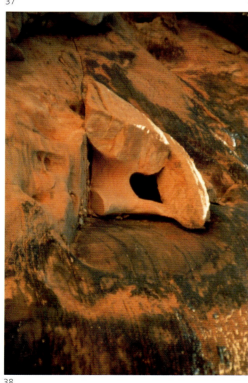

38

39

40

41

42

43

Clark County Government Center 111

Natural Resources Building

Design/Completion 1990/1992
Olympia, Washington
Department of General Administration, State of Washington
Offices and laboratories
325,000 square feet/30,471 square meters (six levels)
Composite steel frame and concrete core, acid-etched precast concrete, stucco, limestone, stone, terrazzo, wood
Region: northwestern United States; temperate zone rain forest
Context: Washington State Capitol complex

Washington State's Natural Resources Building in Olympia, Washington, consolidated the State's forestry, agriculture, and fisheries agencies in a single facility, bringing together its 1,200 employees. The structure reflects these agencies' mission while also melding with the existing Beaux Arts-style architecture of the Washington State Capitol campus. Fentress Bradburn won the commision to design the building in a national competition.

With its gracefully curving 675-foot façade, the Natural Resources Building makes a sweeping gesture to the western Capitol campus, while creating a cornerstone for the eastern campus. It echoes the stately curvature of the Capitol, reinterpreting its columns into slender pillars. Along with the green trusses that cap these along the south façade, these pillars also evoke the trunks of trees—a reference to resources governed by one of the building's agencies. The repetition of "tree" columns also creates a structural canopy that offers a sense of enclosure. The plaza at the east end, which serves as a terminus both for the building's curve and its "forest" of columns, cascades down to a landscaped, park-like setting. With patterns simulating beach, cobbled shore, wetland, grassland and forest fringe, the landscaping emulates the richness of the surrounding context of Washington State.

The focal point of the building is a hexagonal rotunda that is off-center to the building but on-axis with the eastern campus grid. This asymetrical resolution generates a powerful site dynamic. The rotunda was placed at the intersection of the existing street system, providing a point of orientation. Within the rotunda, the user is quickly oriented to the building and its agencies, whose public functions are clustered around and within the rotunda for ease of public access.

1

Energy-efficiency was a primary goal of the design. This includes systems that allow for a mix of natural and artificial lighting in a range from one-third at the perimeter to full lighting levels for spaces deep in the interior of the building. Analog light sensors monitor energy use in conjunction with a campus-wide system. The building's cantilevered overhang on its southern exposure cuts direct solar gain while allowing daylight to be reflected off the plaza and into the interior. Prevailing winds are used to aid in ventilation in an HVAC system whose dampers adjust for up to 100 percent fresh-air intake. Such measures have kept the Natural Resources Building's energy use 30 percent lower than nearby office buildings.

The highest indoor air-quality standards were also enforced with the building. Subcontractors and suppliers were held to stringent materials standards in order to minimize indoor emissions. Prior to being occupied, the entire building was given a 90-day flush-out to rid it of the noxious gases common with new construction.

In 1993, Fentress Bradburn Architects was honored with the Architecture and Energy Building Excellence Award for the design of the Natural Resources Building. The design was evaluated and awarded on the basis of energy performance, treatment of energy-related elements, climatic responsive design, and creativity.

1 Night shot, northeast façade
2 West façade, with atrium
3 Model, showing alignment of building with State Capitol
4 Site plan

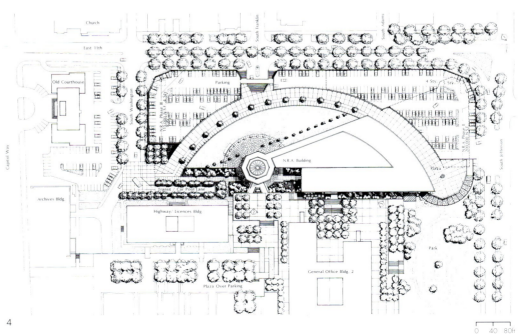

Natural Resources Building

5 Floor plans from main (bottom) to uppermost levels (top)
6 Green trusses on pillars reference trees.
7 Atrium, as seen from under building overhang
Opposite:
   Northeast façade

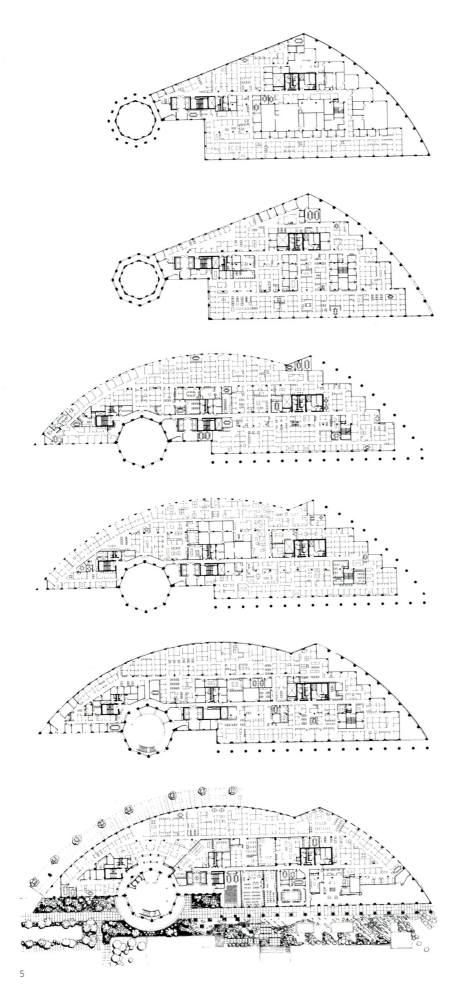

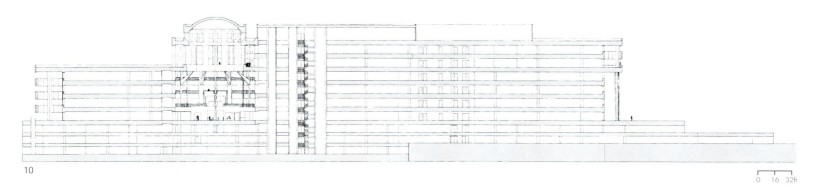

Opposite:
   Atrium brings light deep into the building.
10 Section, south façade
11 Break areas are arranged around light-filled atrium.
12 Rounded forms of atrium welcome visitors.

Natural Resources Building **117**

Larimer County Justice Center

Design/Completion 1999/2000
Fort Collins, Colorado
Government center
170,000 square feet/15,790 square meters
Stone, brick veneer, stucco, metal roofing
Region: western United States
Context: late 19th-century masonry buildings

The goal of the design competition for the Larimer County Justice Center was to create a dignified civic building that would blend with the local historic architecture of Fort Collins, Colorado. Competition sponsors were also hopeful the design could balance this substantial structure with extensive open public space in a way that could be extrapolated to a multiple-block district.

Fentress Bradburn focused on local building conventions that extend buildings to their sites' edges and give them corner entrances, establishing a diagonal orientation. The firm's design sets the lower levels of the building at the site edge, fixing the entrance on the northeastern corner of the site in a hexagonal atrium on a diagonal cut to the two-story, strongly rectilinear base shape. Although the building rises to a height of five stories in an area dominated by two- and four-story buildings, it also demonstrates a respectful prominence by stepping back the top three stories so that the new structure doesn't overwhelm its neighbors. Exterior building materials of sandstone and brick are organized in a pattern that reinforces the two-story base component of the building, while employing above it the brick pilaster and arcade configuration common to the area. The design also echoes the local repetition of vertically proportioned windows to establish strong horizontal lines. A strong civic note is sounded with the light-colored brick pilasters rising to meet strong pediment shapes at the top of the building.

A main public plaza southwest of the courthouse overlooks a park and offers a fountain as well as an amphitheater for lunchtime performances or community gatherings. Created as part of the site plan, a walkway spine running through several interconnecting blocks reinforces the pedestrian scale of both the building and its exterior spaces.

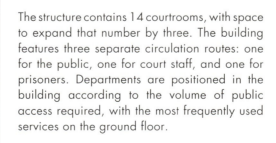

The structure contains 14 courtrooms, with space to expand that number by three. The building features three separate circulation routes: one for the public, one for court staff, and one for prisoners. Departments are positioned in the building according to the volume of public access required, with the most frequently used services on the ground floor.

1   Northeast façade, main entrance
2   Masonry-walled hexagonal atrium
3   Entrance canopy
4   Site plan

Opposite:
Southwest façade, showing arches
6&7 Southwest façade, back entrance
8 Sally port on south façade

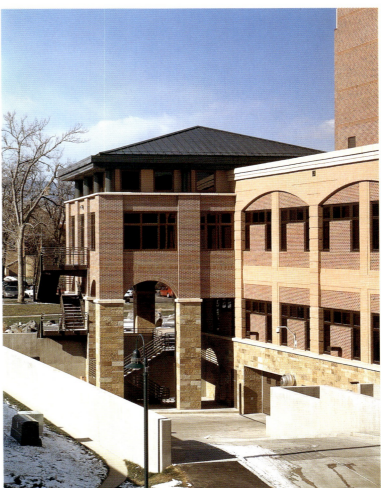

Larimer County Justice Center 121

9 Shallow arch in lower hallway
10 Rounded entry overhang distinguishes County Clerk's office
11 View down into lobby at southwest entrance
12 Courtroom
13 Law library
14 Floor plan, upper levels
15 Floor plan main level

9

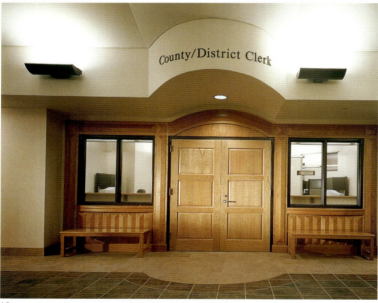

10

12

11

13

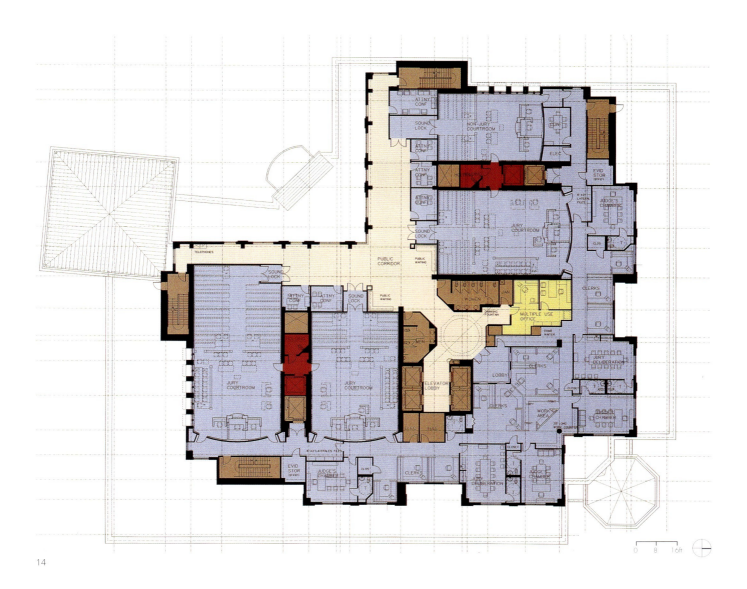

14

15

Larimer County Justice Center **123**

Civic Center Parking Structure

Design/Completion 1998/1999
Fort Collins, Colorado
City of Fort Collins
305,000 square feet/28,335 square meters
900 vehicles
15,080 square feet of street-level retail
Architectural precast, steel and concrete

Fentress Bradburn won the competition to design the four-level, 900-car Civic Center Parking Structure, created to handle the parking needs of the new Larimer County Justice Center, the city office building, and adjacent retail business patrons.

The structure provides 15,000 square feet of retail space at street level, and is designed to blend with adjacent historic storefront properties, disguising its mass behind a series of façades that are individualized by their detailing. Fentress Bradburn's design transforms the bulk and mass of the parking garage into a turn-of-the-century masonry structure in tune with surrounding architecture.

Window proportions and their recessed, rectangular openings give a look of continuity with nearby historic structures. Detailing also links the building to the new Justice Center. Drivers reach the parking areas by way of two 3-lane entrances on different sides of the building. The direction of the center lane can be switched to provide greater ingress or egress, depending on the time of day. A flow-through design minimizes congestion and maintains clear separation between vehicular and pedestrian pathways.

2

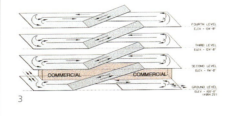
3

4

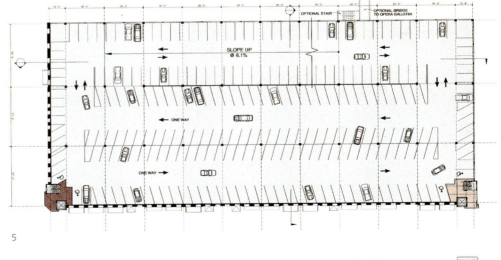
5

6

1

1 Main entrance
2 Side street façade with main pedestrian entrance
3 Section, width
4 Elevation
5 Floor plan
6 Section, length
7 Main street façade, with differentiated storefronts
8 Alley entrance, with bridge to shopping gallery at right

Civic Center Parking Structure 125

La Nueva Área Terminal del Aeropuerto Madrid/Barajas (New Terminal Area for Madrid/Barajas International Airport)

1997
Madrid, Spain
Aeropuertos Espanoles y Navegacion Aerea
Airport
39,700,000 square feet/368,851 square meters
38 gates, 36 million passengers annually
Concrete, steel, glass, tensile fabric
Region: western Mediterranean
Context: existing airport

A high-tech solution brings ancient forms to life in Fentress Bradburn's 1997 design submission for the new Terminal Area of the Madrid–Barajas Airport.

Capitalizing on the play of light at Madrid's latitude, the design weds a tensile fabric roof to the arch shape typical of Spanish architecture. From the exterior, the structure has the white, opaque look characteristic of Mediterranean building. On the inside, the fabric roof diffuses light to the interior, giving it a luminous quality and making the space inside light and airy. Large glass curtainwalls at each end of the terminal, plus clerestories at regular intervals in the roof, mix diffuse light with direct light, giving travelers a clear sense of time of day.

The roof itself rises in a gentle sequence of waves to cover the large arched space of the Great Hall. This arched, fabric-covered latticework, and the columns and arched forms within the ticketing area and the Great Hall, serve both as structural members and as representations of traditional Spanish architecture. Shades, cloisters, loggias, interior patios, galleries, pergolas, and screens also mirror building conventions of the Iberian peninsula, including both Moorish and Roman influences.

Flooring alternates between carpeted rest areas and native granite. The earthy palette of interior colors is drawn from contextual materials on the plains of Madrid, and ranges from ocher to burnt sienna.

1 Model view of terminal, from tarmac
2 Floor plan, linear concourse at right
3 Computer rendering with lighted terminal
4 Model, from approach roads

1

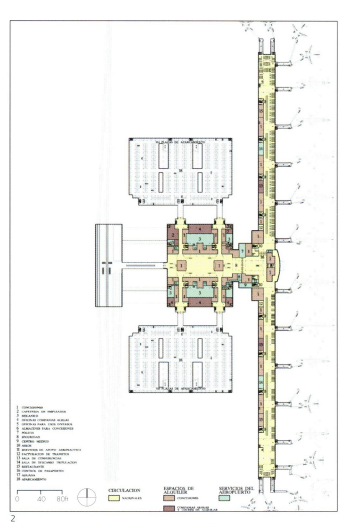

La Nueva Área Terminal del Aeropuerto Madrid/Barajas 127

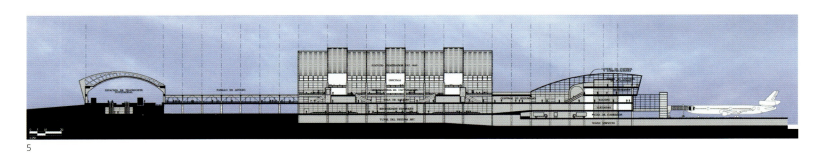

5

7

5 Section through Great Hall, landside to airside
6 Section of Great Hall
7 Night view from tarmac, arched Great Hall at back

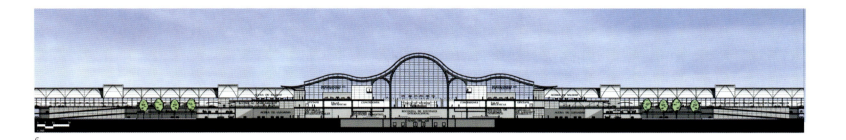

6

La Nueva Área Terminal del Aeropuerto Madrid/Barajas

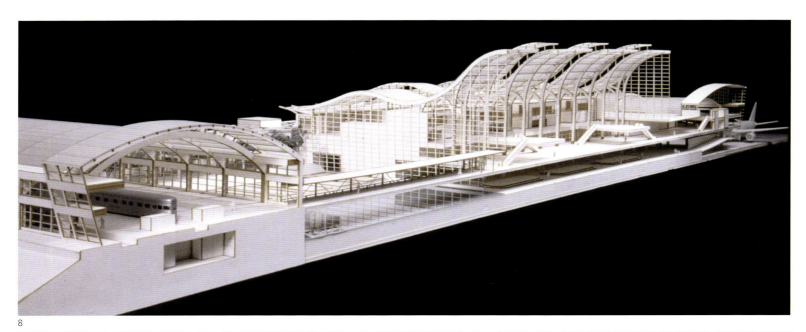

8

9

8   Model section, train station at left
9   Model interior, Great Hall, with arches under fabric roof
10 Rendering, ticket hall interior
Right:
    Rendering, interior of Great Hall

130

10

Flughafen Wien
(Vienna Airport Expansion)

1999
Vienna, Austria
Airport expansion
addition of 24 gates, doubling of ticketing hall,
master plan for environs around airport
development

Fentress Bradburn won honorable mention in the international competition to design the terminal complex expansion of Vienna International Airport. The firm was invited to compete with 15 other architects in a program that called for doubling the size of the existing terminal and adding 24 gates.

The site's perimeter is a circular access road which already links many of the airport's components. Instead of filling up this circular space, Fentress Bradburn sought to condense the program, to compress functions into a singular architectural identity. This would connect the airport with the city master plan in a meaningful way and would create a memorable experience of the site from the nearby *autobahn*.

The result was a long, transparent linear shape the length of the diameter of the circular access road. The structure unifies all buildings on the site, reaching out into the landscape, floating on pilotis so as to give free access from one side of the building to the other. It is six stories in height, and links travelers to car-rental returns, parking garages, and retail concessions, as well as to the airport's main ticketing hall, baggage claim, and concourses. The design also provides for 215,000 square feet (19,974 square meters) of office space on the upper floors and at the end of the building that is farthest from the airport.

Inside the structure, as travelers leave the parking garages, they have only one direction in which to go in order to reach ticketing and concourses. Visitors move along the transparent side of the building, having open views of the landscape and ready access to retail outlets. The open metal lacework that encases the building is not only aesthetically stimulating but also frames views of the landscape and functions as a sun-shading device.

1

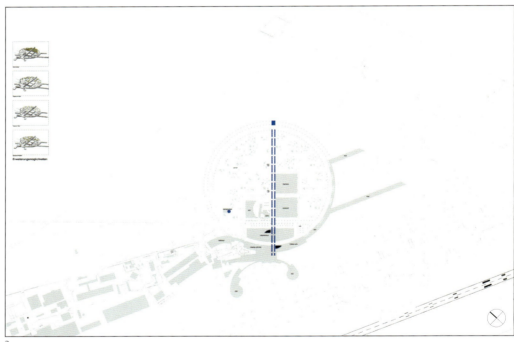

2

By compressing function into a single line across the site, the design frees up the landscape, which can then be returned to nature—an amenity rarely found in airports. The quiet, simple shape of the building, realized in a soothing blue, catches the eye from a distance—an instantly recognizable icon for the city of Vienna.

1 West façade, from northwest angle
2 Site plan
3 East façade, from southeast; new gates at middle
4 Linear shape at back connects with existing curved concourse in foreground.
5 Model, showing circular access road
6 Floor plans
7 Floor plans showing new gates that curve with access road

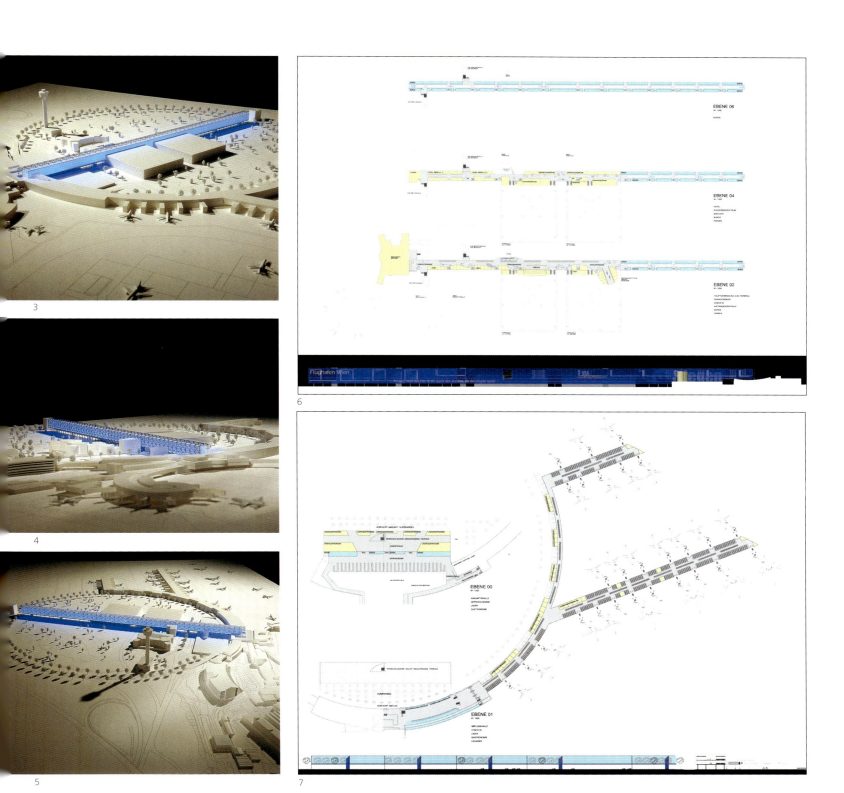

The Hughes Center

Design/Completion 1995/1999
Las Vegas, Nevada
The Howard Hughes Corporation
Speculative office buildings
3883 Howard Hughes Parkway 12 stories, 209,475 square feet/19,460 square meters
3993 Howard Hughes Parkway 8 stories, 185,000 square feet/17,187 square meters
3790 Howard Hughes Parkway 9 stories, 210,00 square feet/19,509 square meters
Granite, glass, stone, wood
Region: western United States
Context: office park

Fentress Bradburn won two competitions to design speculative office buildings at The Hughes Center, a Class A office park owned, developed, and managed by The Howard Hughes Corporation, and located about a mile off The Strip in Las Vegas, Nevada. The firm was then commissioned to design a third building.

3883 Howard Hughes Parkway
The first competition, in 1995, was a four-week design charrette for a 12-story office tower located off the key intersection of Corporate Drive and Howard Hughes Parkway. The building—a Class A speculative, high-rise office tower—is a focal point for the office park, greeting visitors from the end of the entry axis as they turn into The Hughes Center.

A lobby rotunda protrudes in a soft curvilinear shape at the center of the building, reinforcing the gentle curve of Howard Hughes Parkway. The granites used on the exterior are carried into the building on the walls and floors of the two-story interior lobby. The building's flexibility is seen in the corporate front doors that ground-floor tenants enjoy in addition to direct access through the main lobby.

The building connects to a parking structure by way of an open shaded arcade which defines a special outdoor entry courtyard, complete with sculpture and a formal palm alleé that leads to the building's entry. On-grade visitor parking accommodates 90 cars, with structured employee parking for 610 cars.

3993 Howard Hughes Parkway
This 1998 competition was a shorter, less formal charrette than the first. Many of the design characteristics of the first structure influenced the design of the second. The exterior of this 8-story, Class A, multi-tenant office building is clad in Baltic brown granite, with a two-story polished granite base. A

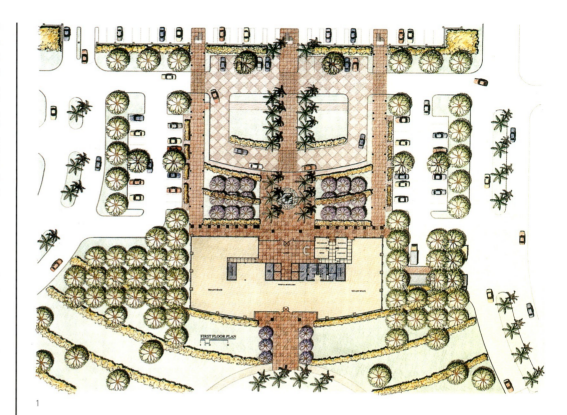

1

2   3

two-story entry rotunda was designed with interior finishes in granite, limestone, and wood, to create a dramatic and elegant greeting for visitors. The curvilinear form at the entryway continues up the full 8 floors, creating bay windows that give panoramic views back to The Las Vegas Strip and to the mountains beyond. Floor-to-ceiling glass at all office locations provides for excellent views in all directions.

3790 Howard Hughes Parkway
Fentress Bradburn was commissioned to design this speculative, 9-story, 210,000-square-foot building on one of the last sites available at The Hughes Center. A combination granite-and-glass exterior with punched openings ties the building to other architecture at The Hughes Center, while a dramatic frontal image facing the parkway gives the building a timeless elegance. The interior of the main lobby is of stone and wood. Green space at the front of the building will provide The Hughes Center with a new, park-like commons area.

1   Site plan, 3883 Howard Hughes Parkway
2   Model, 3883 at center, 3970 at top, 3993 at bottom
3   Model, aerial, 3883 on axis with entry into Hughes Center
4   3993 Howard Hughes Parkway
5   Floor plans for 3883 Howard Hughes Parkway

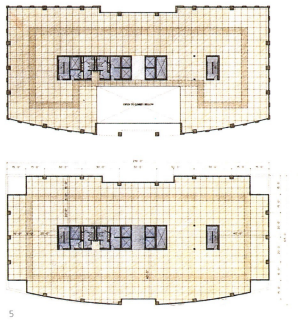

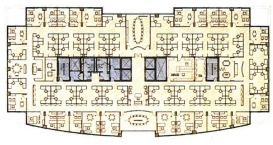

The Hughes Center 135

6   3993 Howard Hughes Parkway

The Hughes Center

Opposite:
3993 Howard Hughes Parkway
8   Elevations, details, 3883 Howard Hughes Parkway
9   Rendering, front plaza, 3883 Howard Hughes Parkway

The Hughes Center   139

10 Model of lobby, 3993 Howard Hughes Parkway
11 Elevator lobby model, 3993 Howard Hughes Parkway
Opposite:
Lobby, 3993 Howard Hughes Parkway

The AEC Design Competition 1996

1996
Long Beach, California
Second Annual AEC Design Competition
Bentley Systems, Inc.
Mixed-use residential and commercial urban design
6 commercial buildings: 3.4 million square feet/
315,860 square meters
5 residential buildings: 1.6 million square feet/
148,640 square meters
6,000 parking spaces
Region: West Coast of the United States
Context: shoreline at the edge of an urban area

1

In July 1996, Fentress Bradburn Architects won the Second Annual AEC Design Competition, which was sponsored by engineering software maker Bentley Systems, Inc. The task was to design a mixed-use residential and commercial redevelopment of a 13-acre seaside property at Long Beach, California. The site had formerly been home to an amusement park, and was one of the largest remaining parcels of coastal urban real estate in the country. The challenge was to create an area that would help promote Long Beach as a major West Coast commercial center while closely intermingling commercial and residential functions on the site.

Fentress Bradburn defined this as an opportunity to create an interface between a rectilinear urban grid and the dynamic, undulating edge of the oceanfront. When any two disparate patterns intersect, the result is a third entity, with similarities to its originators, but arranged in its own unique rhythm.

As the complex approaches the ocean edge, the rectilinear pattern of movement and development in downtown Long Beach begins to shift and skew within the project site. The resultant radial pattern of streets and building lots naturally creates parks, plazas, and other open areas. The concept of shifting patterns is also explored in the building masses and façades. The buildings themselves start with simple floor plates at the lower floors and evolve into more complex forms as the exterior skin is manipulated to form inclined and stepped planes.

2

3

Most similar to their urban neighbors, and sited closest to the city, are commercial buildings which house offices and hotels. Next to these are residential buildings which begin at medium height and step down to the ocean. The tall buildings form a distinctive skyline and a backdrop to the mid-rise residential developments fronting the shoreline.

Among secondary design challenges were the slope of the site and requirements for parking. The firm's design accommodates the 16-foot drop from the city side to the ocean side of the site by using steps, ramps, and terraces. Fentress Bradburn accomodates the 6,000 parking spaces called for by terracing them under the plaza so that parking is close and convenient but out of sight.

The residential buildings are laid out in a radiating pattern and step down towards the ocean, forming the transition from mid- to low-rise. This configuration allows for greater ocean views from the units, and also maximizes sun penetration into the site. As the buildings step down, they engage the edge of the garage

142

structure, forming recognizable portals into the parking levels, and framing ramps or staircases for pedestrian access to the plaza.

Further underscoring the concept of movement and change, the façades of the residential buildings are subtly skewed, with the different planes being clad in cool tones of glass or fashioned in warmer tones of stucco. The landscape echoes a similar configuration. Paving and planting shift patterns as they move across the site and are overlaid with gestures of swoops and trajectories associated with amusement park rides and structures, referencing the site's previous use.

The design offers residents a choice of 15 floor plans in studios, one-bedroom and two-bedroom units with balconies and terraces that offer ocean views, as well as such amenities as spas, pools, and a fitness center.

Fentress Bradburn was chosen from among a field of three finalists which included Cooper Carry & Associates of Atlanta, Georgia, and Tao and Lee of St. Louis, Missouri. Judges included Los Angeles architects Annie Chu of Chu+Gooding, and Katherine Diamond of Siegel Diamond, as well as Jim Russell, senior editor of *Architectural Record*.

1 Elevations on presentation boards
2 Computer rendering, detail from ocean side of complex
3 Computer rendering of entire site
4 Site plan

Cathedral City Civic Center

1995
Cathedral City, California
City hall and police station
50,000 square feet/4,645 square meters
Natural stone, concrete, steel, wood and stucco
Region: Palm Springs desert
Context: older, very small downtown with suburban scale
Guiding metaphor: palm trees and Native American ceremonial roundhouse

Desert imagery from the environs of Cathedral City, California, guided Fentress Bradburn's design of the city's proposed new civic center. The opportunity arose when the firm was asked to participate in a competition to design a civic complex encompassing a city hall and police station—the first major public improvement in the town's downtown area.

Fentress Bradburn's design leads visitors by way of a pedestrian promenade through a sequence of spaces between the town's bell tower and the new civic structure. Once through the final oasis of the town square, the visitor is greeted by two ceremonial gateways—the council chambers and the atrium, a shaded structure that is not enclosed but is open to the sky.

The rising trusses of the atrium evoke the lofty peaks of the nearby San Jacinto Mountains, while its lattice work resembles the leaves of a palm frond. The form of the council chambers is derived from the *kishumnawut*, the Cahuilla Native American ceremonial roundhouse of the Coachella Valley. Its roof takes a form reminiscent of the flowering barrel cactus.

The three-story plan enhances accessibility by locating the city's public service counters on the ground floor, directly off the atrium. The council chamber is maintained as the house of government. A large window looking into the chambers from the colonnade speaks to democratic ideals of a government of the people.

The design accommodates the area's harsh desert climate by using shading structures and recessed windows to reduce solar heat gain. The shaded colonnade running the length of the Third Street façade offers a contemporary interpretation of an ancient building tradition. Water is used sparingly, as a canal alongside the pedestrian promenade, ending with a sheltered fountain in the Cathedral City atrium. A separate wall of water in the town square evokes the image of a desert seep and minimizes the spray that could be kicked up by desert winds if a traditional fountain were used.

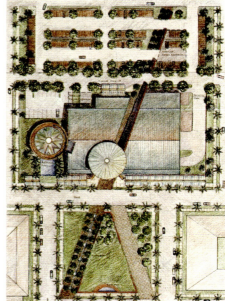

1 Rendering of atrium
2 Site plan; atrium at center, council chamber at left
3 Floor plan of complex

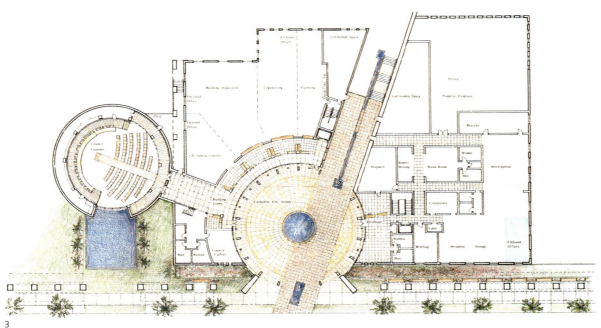

Cathedral City Civic Center

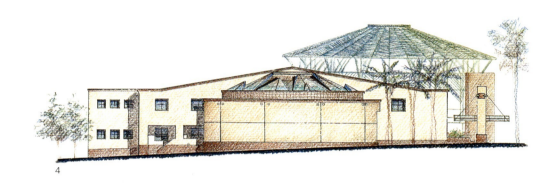

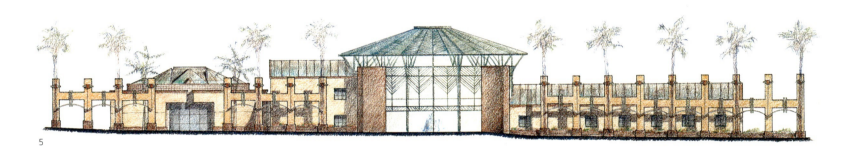

4 Elevation, north façade
5 Elevation, west façade, atrium at center
6 Model, as seen from southeast angle
7 Model detail
8 Elevation, south façade
9 Elevation east façade
10 Atrium model
11 Atrium model interior, detail

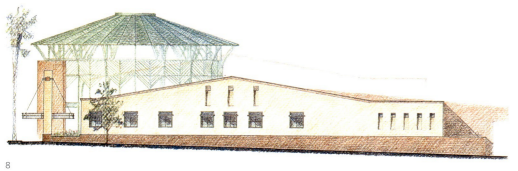
8

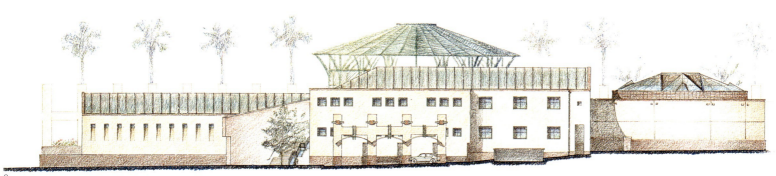
9

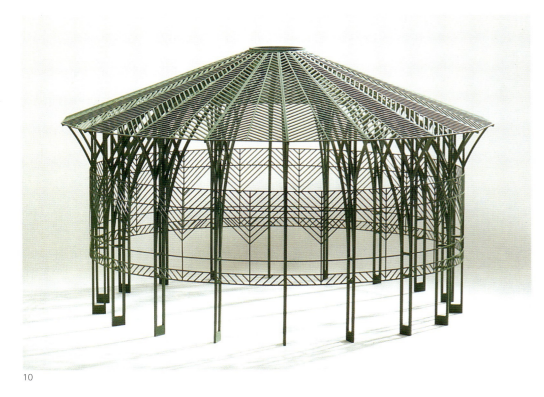
10

11

Cathedral City Civic Center **147**

Special Projects

National Museum of Wildlife Art

Design/Completion 1993/1994
Jackson, Wyoming
Museum
35,365 square feet/3,285 square meters
Steel frame, concrete, stone, glass, gypsum, carpet
Region: western United States
Context: rocky bluff
Guiding metaphor: regeneration

Numerous ecological issues had to be solved in order to create the National Museum of Wildlife Art. The 70-acre site on which the museum was to be erected had been brutalized over time by mining and ranching interests in the area, and later by a commercial campground. A large part of the land had been leveled to make three giant shelves on which trailers could be parked. There was a desire to reclaim the scarred hillside and to make the museum unobtrusive, especially since it overlooks the National Elk Reserve and is close to both the Grand Tetons and Yellowstone National Park.

Fentress Bradburn created a building that is masked as a rock outcropping, a structure that looks partly like antique miners' cabins and partly like castle ruins, but which blends into the background of the bluff into which it is built. The museum sits on one of the three shelves that marred the site, while using another shelf for parking. Cars are obscured from onlookers across the open valley by way of a landscaped berm. The site's third shelf was returned to natural grade and native grasses, with the idea of attracting wildlife native to the area, including mule deer, foxes, and rabbits.

The museum is built into the hillside of the East Gros Ventre Bluff. The building twists with the topography, pivoting at a gulch that creases the hill. Designers were able to bring this line through the building by re-directing the site's drainage to it in order to maintain the foliage growing along the gulch as it descends the hill below the museum. This channeling of moisture was accomplished without permitting any visible flashing on the building. The flashing is concealed beneath the stone cladding—a feature that helps the building blend into its background and, in a sense, allows the building to touch the sky in a very natural way.

The museum is reached by a circuitous route that permits it to emerge as a building and then fade into the background as the visitor approaches, evoking the experience of wildlife observation itself. Stone cladding gives the building its mutable appearance. When the visitor finally reaches the structure, all that is encountered is a stone wall and a peaked canopy made of the trunks of stripped-bark pine trees that were salvaged from the Yellowstone Fire of 1988.

Visitors enter the museum from a cascading stone stairway leading down into a canyon-like lobby which affords spectacular views of the surrounding mountains and valley. The galleries themselves are secluded in the hillside interior portion of the building in order to manage light and humidity issues that could affect the collection.

1 Museum exterior emulates rocky outcropping above.
2 Museum from across the valley
3 Winter shot with rock outcroppings behind building
4 Site plan

3

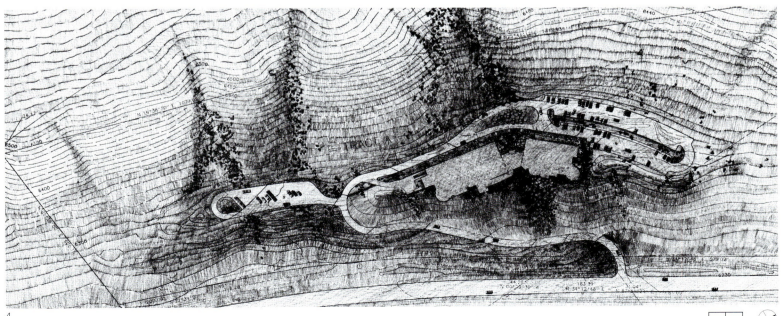

4

Previous pages:
Stone-clad exterior helps museum blend into its background.
6   Patio enclosure for bronze sculpture at left
7   Winter shot of bronze bear and valley below
8   Stone cladding harmonizes museum with its setting.
9   Rendering

6

7

8

10   Section showing view plane and seasonal solar penetration
11   Peaked canopy and stone wall at entry level
Opposite:
     Canopy's timbers were salvaged from 1988 Yellowstone Fire.

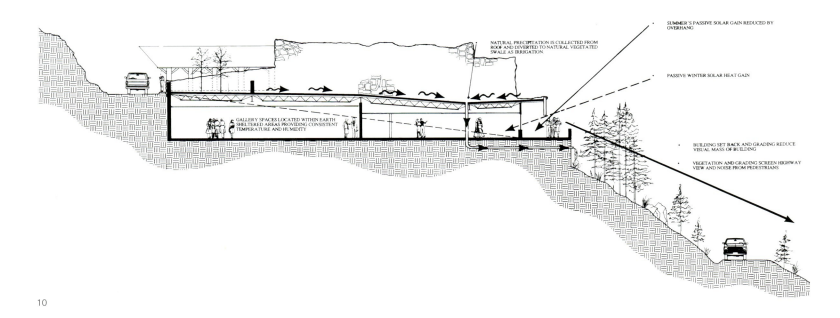

10

11

13

14

13 Bronze mountain lion guards canyon-like lobby.
14 Visitors enter by way of stone stairway.
15 Animal tracks are etched into floor of lobby.
16 Floor plan

15

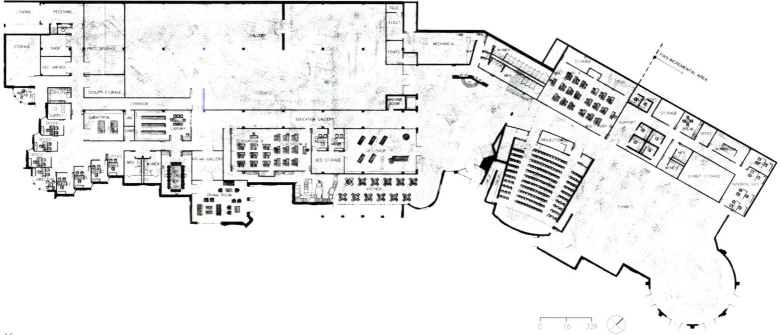
16

National Museum of Wildlife Art 159

17

18

17 Lounge
18 Conference room
Opposite:
   Entry to administrative wing

20

21

22

23

20 Totem pole is lit from above by skylight.
21 Demonstration area
22 Bronze buffalo
23 Gallery space

24

25

24 Sculptures include turtles (foreground) and dolphins.
25 Gallery near demonstration area
26 Exhibit area
27 Sculptures are prominently displayed in galleries.

National Museum of Wildlife Art 165

Denver International Airport Passenger Terminal

Design/Completion 1991/1994
Denver, Colorado
City and County of Denver
Airport
2,000,000 square feet/185,800 square meters, parking structure: 12,000 spaces, administration: 250,000 square feet/23,225 square meters
94 gates, 32 million passengers annually
Architectural precast concrete, composite steel frame, precast concrete, glass, steel cables, Teflon-coated fiberglass fabric, granite, stainless steel
Region: western United States
Context: juncture of mountain and plain
Guiding metaphor: the Rocky Mountains

The soaring, "snow-capped" peaks of Denver International Airport's passenger terminal, inspired by the jagged profile of the nearby Rocky Mountains, created an iconographic symbol for the city of Denver. A gateway to the West, Denver International Airport is known widely for its innovative design and unique sense of place, as well the sense of lift its interior confers on visitors.

The building's tensile-membrane fabric roof is configured into 34 peaks that are held aloft on columns up to 150 feet tall. So much light penetrates the translucent fabric roof that artificial lighting is required only at night, at which time the roof becomes a beacon on the plains. This natural daylighting has reduced both lighting and cooling costs of the structure, resulting in significant energy savings. It also permits the growth of abundant plant life within the terminal, enhancing the intimate seating areas spaced throughout. This light is augmented by direct light from the 60-foot-high, 220-foot-wide glass curtainwall at the building's southern end, where the wing-like spans of the roof's end panels frame spectacular views.

The Great Hall within this space conjures up the grandeur of the great railway stations of a century ago, and the romance that once was—and still should be—associated with travel. The open and expansive design is clear and straightforward, with subtle reinforcing elements. The two bridges that traverse the cathedral-like space help to orient travelers, signaling where they need to descend in order to catch trains to the concourses. Other orientation aids include the "paper planes" hanging sculpture in the main terminal train station, which directs arriving passengers to baggage claim areas, and the directional patterns in the granite floors which help to channel passengers from ticketing to trains and from trains to baggage claim areas.

1

2

The largest fully enclosed, integrated tensile-fabric structure in the world when it was built, Denver International Airport is now second in size only to the Millennium Dome.

In 1995, the design of Denver International Airport earned Fentress Bradburn the Design Honor Award of the United States Department of Transportation.

3

4

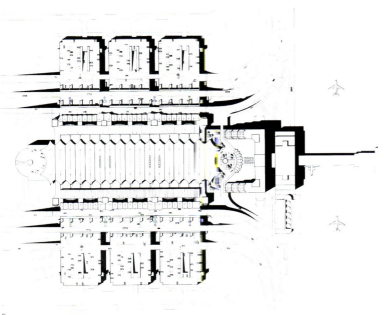

5

1 Aerial view from north side, Concourse A in foreground
2 Ground view from northeast angle
3 Winter sunset behind terminal
4 Night view, east façade
5 Site plan

Denver International Airport Passenger Terminal **167**

6   South façade at dusk
7   Section of skylighted mast top
8   Southwest façade, with four of the eight skylighted mast tops
Opposite:
    Lower peaks frame glass curtainwall at south end.

6

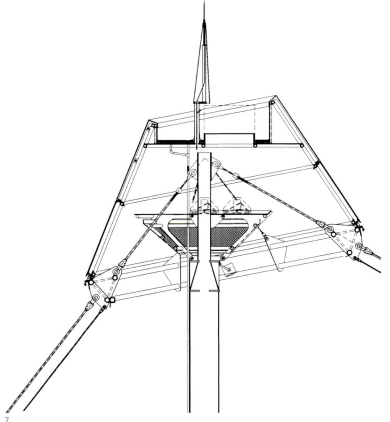

7

8

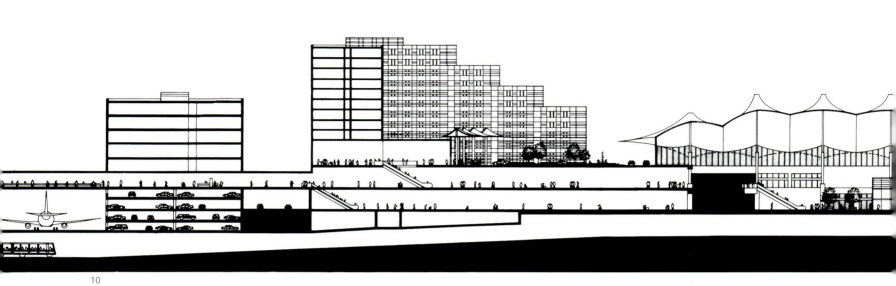
10

11

12

10 Section of terminal
11 Interior of Great Hall
12 Lamp sculptures emulate shape of masts.
13 Clerestories allow direct light to penetrate into Great Hall.
14 External mast, northern end of terminal

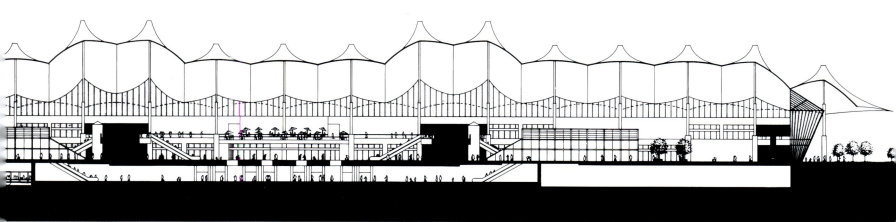

Denver International Airport Passenger Terminal 171

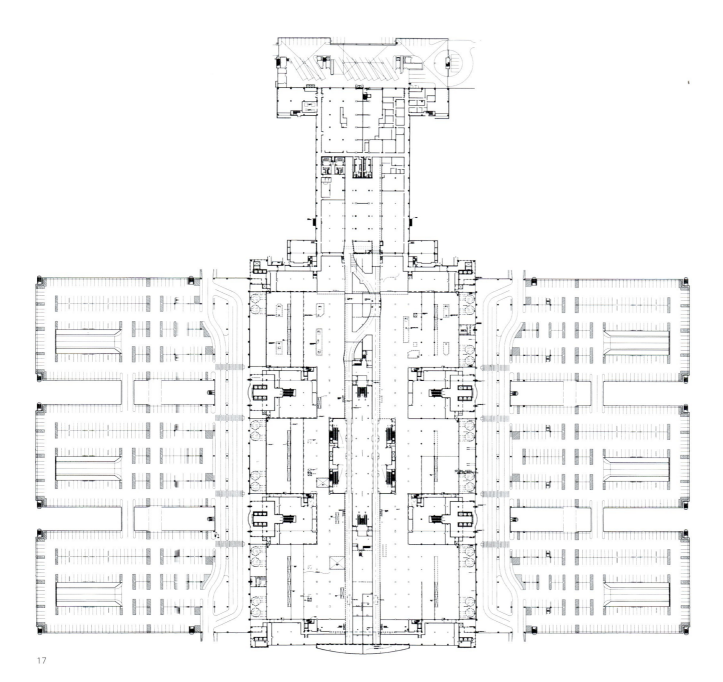

Previous pages:
    Glass curtainwall at south end of terminal
Opposite:
    Ceiling shape echoes compass rose on floor of train station.
17   Floor plan, train level; parking garages at left and right
18   Baggage claim area
19   "Paper planes" direct arriving passengers to baggage claim.

Denver International Airport Passenger Terminal **175**

The Denver Permit Center

Design/Completion 1987/1989
Denver, Colorado
City and County of Denver
Civic architecture
73,000 square feet/6,782 square meters
Brick, stucco and glass
Region: western United States
Context: cluster of civic structures around a park

Located at a prominent corner of Denver's Civic Center Park, this structure was originally built in 1961 as the University of Denver Law Library. It was done in a modernist style with an exterior system of panels that emphasized the box-like shape of the building. The entryway was not clearly marked structurally, but more importantly, the building did not in any way blend with neighboring architecture or the Civic Center environment.

When the Law Library was relocated to another part of town, the City and County of Denver obtained the building and decided to consolidate within it all of its permitting agencies, which had been scattered around the city. The idea was to create a one-stop permitting facility that would blend into its environs. Recognizing the inappropriate style of the building in such a prominent civic location, Fentress Bradburn Architects chose to revise the building's exterior and to bring it into the family of neoclassical revival structures that characterize Civic Center Park.

The building was renovated to accommodate approximately 250 employees from the departments of building inspection, excise and licenses, planning, zoning administration, and traffic engineering. The exterior skin was reworked to blend better with Denver's City and County Building, which sits directly across the street from it, while also echoing the playful curves of the nearby Gio Ponti-designed Denver Art Museum. Exterior color and detailing transformed the building's character and added civic dignity.

A full-height rotunda at the corner gives the building focus and makes the entryway clear for both pedestrian and vehicular approaches. Lawns and linden trees also emphasize the entry and tie the site to Civic Center Park, which lies in close proximity.

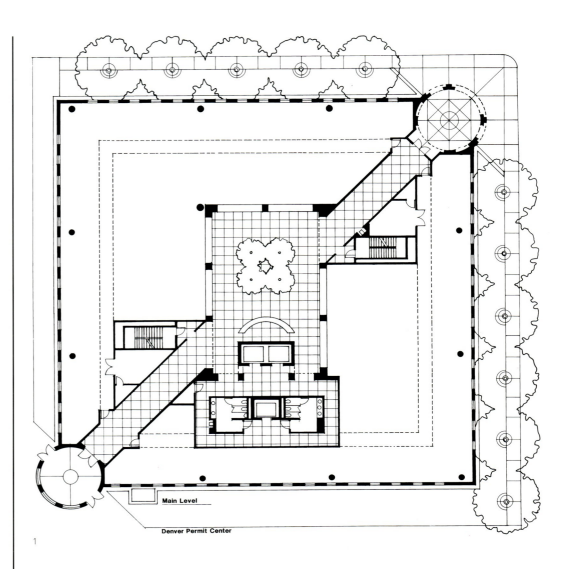

1   Floor plan, main level
2   Building before renovation
3   Permit Center between museum (left), city/county building (right)
4   Building lines echo playful curves of nearby museum.

The building's orientation was reconfigured along a diagonal circulation system, in order to provide better direction for patrons, and to introduce a human scale lacking in the grandiose neoclassicism of the City and County Building. The existing interior space was enclosed and reshaped to create a three-story interior atrium which serves as the central gathering and orientation node of the building, allowing easy accessibility to the most frequently used public permitting services.

Denver's Percent For Art program permitted the installation of two works of art in the building: a suspended stainless steel and neon light sculpture, which hangs in the rotunda entry, and a colorful urban landscape mural, which forms a backdrop to the atrium information desk.

The Denver Permit Center

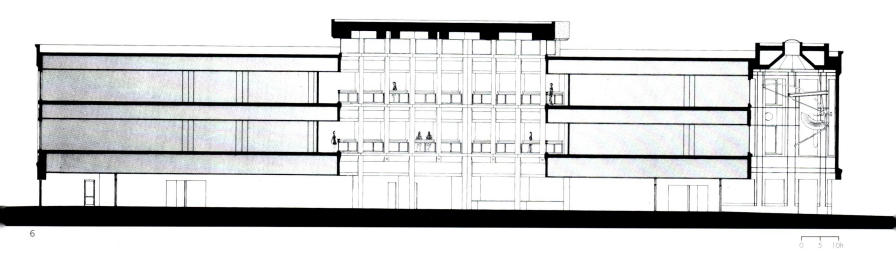

Opposite:
   Three-story atrium at information desk in center of building
6 Section, east façade
7 Atrium exterior, detail
8 Atrium ceiling with sculpture

The Tritch Building Renovation and The Rialto Café

Design/Completion 1996/1998
Denver, Colorado
Sage Hospitality Resources
Hotel and restaurant
hotel six stories plus conference level, 180 hotel rooms, 127,000 square feet/11,798 square meters
café 6,800 square feet/632 square meters
Steel, concrete, wood, plaster, brick, granite
Region: Great Plains at the foot of the Rocky Mountains
Context: downtown urban pedestrian mall with other historic structures
Guiding concept: return the building to its original dignity

Built in 1887, this historic building housed the downtown location of Joslin's, a Denver department store chain, from 1900 to 1992. The renovation and restoration of the building converted the store to a 180-room Courtyard by Marriott hotel.

In 1927, the building went through the first of its many face-lifts with the addition of a fifth floor. Also during this time, the existing small windows were cut out and replaced with large, Chicago-style windows that are currently seen on the building. In 1964, an exterior panel system was installed over the entire outside surface of the building, with the department store's logo emblazoned across it. This cladding modernized the building in line with architectural trends then sweeping the nation. Also at this time, a five-floor addition was attached to the southern side of the building. The cladding camouflaged the new addition, a plain brick box, and gave the entire structure a unified appearance.

The 1964 cladding extensively damaged many of the original building's historic features, including exterior masonry and windows. The 1996 conversion and renovation undertook repairs of this damage as well as a re-design which punched openings for large Chicago-style windows in the walls of the brick-box addition. This and the extension of similar cornice treatments along the length of the building gave the addition a unified look with the adjacent historic façade.

The renovation added a 6th floor to the building, incorporating four suites with terraces. This addition and the creation of an interior, full-height atrium required extensive structural re-engineering of the entire building. The upgrade increased the footing size, reinforced columns and beams, tied the floors to the exterior walls, and re-built the existing

roof. The basement was converted into a conference center with a restaurant, pool, fitness center, and hotel support spaces. The dramatic interior atrium, which is topped by a 40 x 40-foot skylight, reaches from the conference level, which is below grade, through the new top of the building.

Among new first-floor tenants is The Rialto Café, named for the cinema built next door to The Tritch Building in the 1920s. Fentress Bradburn Architects worked with J. Kattman Associates on the interior design for The Rialto.

In keeping with the historic character of the building, the restaurant was done in an Art Deco style. In order to increase the dining area, a mezzanine was added. But with a ceiling height of only 16 feet, the space required a unique design of structural, mechanical, and lighting systems to achieve maximum clearance and to incorporate a smoke exhaust system for the upper level cigar lounge.

Given Colorado's often mild winter weather, Concept Restaurants, the client, required windows in the historic façade to be operable so that the café could have an open-air feel. However, the Colorado Historical Society would not permit the 8 x 5-foot windows to be divided further. Fentress Bradburn created a framing system which allows each window to pivot at its center and slide to the edge of the opening—an economical solution that satisfied all parties.

1 Building section, northwest façade
2 Historic photo after 1927 modifications
3 North corner, just before removal of cladding system
4 Post-renovation shot, from pedestrian mall
5 Rialto Café

The Tritch Building Renovation and The Rialto Café

Opposite:
Second-floor view of atrium cut into center of building
7   Main floor lobby
8   Atrium is topped by 40 x 40-foot skylight
9   Floor plan, typical floor

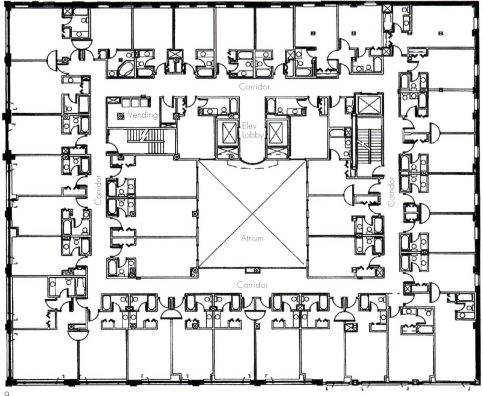

The Tritch Building Renovation and The Rialto Café   183

Temple Sinai

Design/Completion 1984/1987
Denver, Colorado
Temple Sinai congregation
Jewish synagogue
22,000 square feet/2,044 square meters
Smooth and rusticated buff masonry, burgundy ceramic cornice tiles, wood, plaster, glass, stained glass
Guiding metaphor: the temple of King Solomon

The Temple Sinai congregation had worshipped together for 18 years, but never really had a home of its own. The congregation had bought an old elementary school and wanted to create a sanctuary and social space on its western side. The question was how to communicate in architecture such things as spirituality and community—in a sense, to determine the "codes" that signify a religious structure.

The design produced a comfortable, unpretentious yet quietly elegant worship space. The monumental barrel-vaulted entry is designed to be reminiscent of the temple of King Solomon, with lighted, free-standing columns to each side, and a semi-circular, stained-glass window at the end of the vault.

This stained-glass window, visible from outside the temple, brings daylight into the foyer. Designed by a member of the congregation, Helen Ginsburg, and cast by artist Vincent O'Brien of Colorado Springs, the window portrays a story with special significance for Temple Sinai: in the midst of a burning bush are Hebrew letters that state, "And the bush was not consumed."

The stately columns of the lobby give a monumental and classical feel to the space, yet the colors of green and gold, drawn from the colors of the Judean hills, are earthy and inviting.

Among the greatest challenges of the building was to make the interior space flexible enough to accommodate everything from a small wedding to a dinner for 500, to a congregation of 1,600 on the High Holy Days. The design's movable walls allow for the reduction or expansion of the central inner sanctuary, just as its movable pews allow for seating flexibility. The circular floor plate of the sanctuary assures that congregants remain close to the pulpit and the Ark. Clerestory windows around the circumference of the sanctuary bring natural day-lighting into the space.

1 Rendering, west façade
2 Interior of lobby, looking west
3 Floor plan
4 Entry with barrel-vault roof

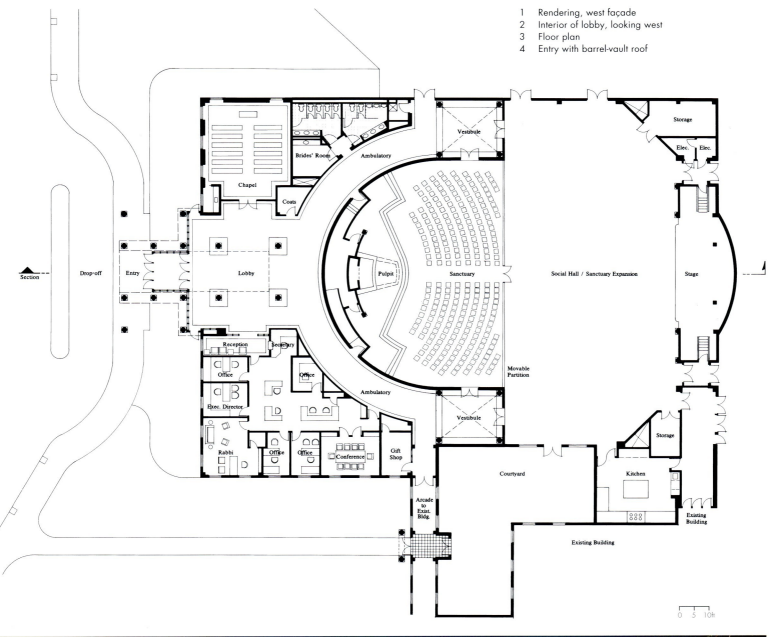

3

4

Temple Sinai 185

5

6

7

5 White columns frame doors to sanctuary.
6 Sanctuary features circular floor plate.
7 Stained-glass sculpture welcomes visitors.

Palmetto Bay Beach Resort

Design/Completion 1996/1999
Roatan, Honduras
Roatan Development Group
Resort
110 acres with a 14-acre village center
55 residential lots for hillside villas (1.5 acres on average), 45 lots for beach houses, 96,000 square feet/8,918 square meters restaurant, pier and hotel
Tropical hardwoods
Region: Caribbean
Context: tropical rainforest

Roatan Island, one of the Bay Islands of Honduras, is one of the most beautiful natural environs of the Caribbean and one of its last unspoiled beachfront settings. Palmetto Bay Beach Resort on Roatan is a small, privately developed resort of 55 hillside villa sites, and a village center with 45 tightly clustered beach houses, located on a 700-foot stretch of palm-lined white sand beach with direct access to the world's second-largest coral reef.

In keeping with the relaxed Caribbean lifestyle and a desire for privacy, Fentress Bradburn's design complements the environment. It melds influences from a variety of Roatan Island cultures, such as the indigenous Paya, as well as West African and colonial. The gabled roof and covered porch of the individual villas speaks of Old World design in colonial environments, while simultaneously suggesting the thatched roofs of indigenous architecture.

This peaked-roof style transcends its influences as it is carried through in the design of the clubhouse at the center of the village. This is an open airy space which houses a restaurant and bar, and fronts on the resort's freshwater swimming pool. It is the focal point of the resort village, a central gathering place. The building is composed primarily of a high peaked roof, part of whose structural support is a series of timbers articulated in diamond shapes at regular intervals from back to front. This transmutes the indigenous *barbacoa* (braided twigs) architecture into a simple, elegant look which makes the space harmonious with the natural setting. Screened louvered doors on all sides can be made to stand open so that air moves freely through the space.

The basic design of all buildings follows such tropical conventions as raising each structure a couple of feet off the ground, and creating deep overhangs to protect villa decks from the heat and rain. Features such as louvered doors, lattice work, transoms, and high ceilings channel natural breezes while providing daylight and ventilation for every room. Smaller spaces, such as closets, bathrooms, and pantries, are also well-ventilated. Exposed wood ceilings echo the thatched ceilings on which they were modeled. The designers also made an architectural element out of hurricane ties that lash the roof to the house perimeter, creating a pattern of long wooden notches evenly spaced across the inside face of the beam at the top of the perimeter walls.

In order to ensure environmental sustainability, the design stipulated use of native Honduran hardwoods certified by the Rain Forest Alliance. The complex also was constructed using water-conserving plumbing and cisterns. The 55 hillside home sites were organized on the site in such a way as to preserve steep hills, wetlands, and drainage basins, and to return the hillside to its natural tropical vegetation following construction. Each 1,000-square-foot beachfront villa features two bedrooms, two baths, a fully equipped modern kitchen, living area, storage room, and a 400-square-foot covered deck.

The 300-foot-long pier that juts out into Palmetto Bay features a palapa bar at the far end.

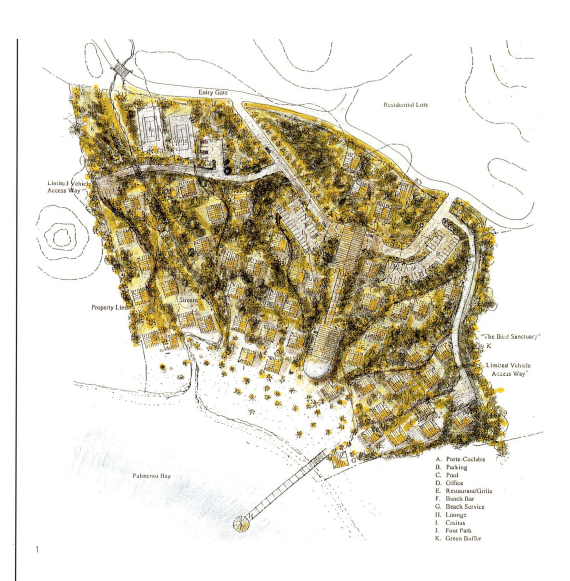

1

1 Site plan
2 Clubhouse
3 Rendering of bay; pier features palapa bar at far end.
4 Beach house

Palmetto Bay Beach Resort **189**

5 Detail, underside of roof overhang
6 Beach house, front façade
7 Bridges connect beach houses.
8 Elevation, showing footings
9 Freshwater swimming pool at clubhouse

IBM Customer Service Center

Design/Completion 1990/1992
Denver Technological Center
Denver, Colorado
International Business Machines Corporation (IBM)
65,000 square feet / 6,093 square meters
Fabric, gypsum, carpet

Spread over three non-contiguous floors, the IBM Customer Service Center called for a design of high-tech presentation rooms, and ease of access necessary for the movement of large groups of people. The client also wanted to project its corporate image of stability and innovation.

The first floor houses a reception area and large presentation classrooms, including a 10,000-square-foot computer room. The third floor is devoted to customer service, with two presentation rooms and four enclosed spaces that have the audio-visual capability to simulate different work situations. Also on this floor are several smaller rooms for one-on-one demonstrations. The fourth floor, a marketing facility that is open to the public for seminars and demonstrations of IBM products, has a guided learning center for classroom training on IBM equipment, in addition to a cafeteria.

In order to seal off light from presentation areas and classrooms on the first and third floors, Fentress Bradburn placed these rooms in the interior of the building, navigating around them with a perimeter corridor that curves inward at important intersections. The corridor gives visitors views of the outside and clarifies for them how the space is organized.

IBM asked that its products be the focal point of the interior design. Fentress Bradburn references the kind of linear, logical thinking associated with computers by bringing inside the grid motif of the exterior windows. The walls opposite the windows of the perimeter corridor mirror this motif, transforming it with

1

curvilinear shapes to suggest creativity and humanistic values. Some grid spaces are only slightly indented, and thus serve as simple walls, while others open as windows into reception and waiting areas. As the corridor curves, the grid spaces deepen enough to display products in interactive demonstration areas.

Furnishings continue the play of angle and curve. Large curvilinear furniture in primary colors of red and blue is juxtaposed against the grid motif for a spontaneous yet sophisticated effect.

2

3

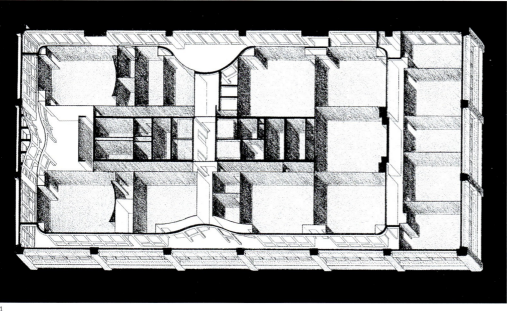

4

1 Employees' cafeteria
2 Break area, marked by curving corridor
3 Reception area
4 Floor plan rendering

5 Product demonstrations fill deeper grid alcoves.
6 Consultation area
7 Waiting area

6

7

The Balboa Company Corporate Headquarters

Design/Completion 1983/1985
Denver, Colorado
The Balboa Company
Corporate interiors
10,000 square feet/929 square meters

The corporate interiors for The Balboa Company, a small investment firm located in the 59th-story penthouse of a downtown Denver office tower, combine the feel of a home and an art gallery without sacrificing the function of an office. The relatively small quarters house a staff of about 15, and were meant to convey a quiet, low-key, unpretentious elegance in line with the company's way of doing business. The client sought to create the atmosphere of a gracious home, with interestingly configured offices and intimate areas for small conferences, and with the firm's extensive collection of contemporary and pre-Colombian art integrated into the environment.

With the penthouse facing to the south, Fentress Bradburn's design takes advantage of the window wall running along the entire length of the offices, emphasizing the sky's proximity and the panoramic views. The floor plan features a series of sharply angled walls that foster a sense of depth and complexity in the limited space. These skewed planes, which are hung with works of art, become focal points, leading visitors more deeply into the space. Each office formed by these angles takes its own individual modified parallelogram shape, just as each is imbued with the occupant's own characteristic style in custom furniture and detailing. A continuous brass hanging track just beneath crown molding at the top of the wall allows for precise placement of paintings. The building's characteristic arc is reflected in cornice work and in the bases of the bookcases. Walls are upholstered in luminous pearl silk bands aligned with the woodwork.

Floors of the reception foyer are white marble inset with black marble squares; elsewhere in the space, flooring ranges from granite to wood parquet and custom woven carpeting.

Visitors enter from the reception area through french doors of Honduran mahogany. Period furniture runs the gamut from late 18th to early 20th century, with the reception foyer dominated by custom reproduction chairs and tables in the Empire style, and English pieces in most executive offices.

State-of-the-art, energy-conserving fixtures are incorporated throughout the offices, including low-voltage, incandescent art-display fixtures and automatic window shades to reduce glare. Sophisticated environmental controls maintain optimum temperature and humidity levels both for occupants and artwork.

1 Cafeteria has penthouse views of mountains.
2 Angled walls give a sense of depth.
3 Conference room with mountain view
4 Waiting area
5 Small conference room
6 Floor plan

4

5

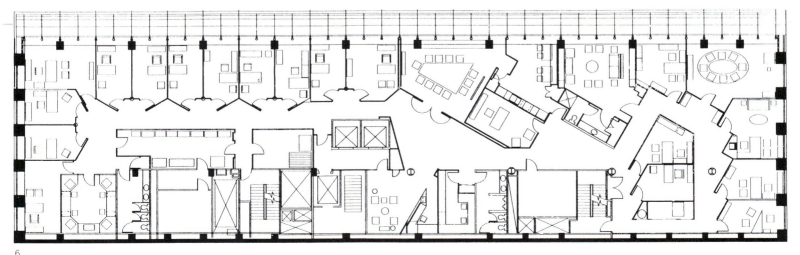

6

Gulf Canada Resources Ltd

Design/Completion 1996/1997
Denver, Colorado
Gulf Canada Resources Ltd
Executive office interiors
50,000 square feet/4,645 square meters
Pine, mahogany, textiles, bronze fittings
Region: western United States
Context: petroleum company's world headquarters

The interiors of Gulf Canada's international operations headquarters are a unique combination of museum galleries and executive office space. Gulf Canada occupies the top two-and-a-half floors of Philip Johnson's Norwest Bank Building in downtown Denver. The company wanted not only to house Gulf Canada's executive senior staff and support personnel, but also its museum-quality Western art collection.

Gulf Canada acquired its unique collection of Native American and Western artifacts and images to reflect the company's creativity, entrepreneurial spirit, and vision. In order to properly house and showcase its many rare pieces, Fentress Bradburn created a warm, comfortable, home-like atmosphere, incorporating colors, materials, and furnishings reminiscent of the West.

Walls are painted the color of wheat grass, recalling the Great Plains and providing a warm, neutral background for paintings, artifacts, and other exhibits. Flooring is predominantly light, old-growth 5-inch-wide pine planks, a warm background for the company's numerous impressive Indian rugs. Other details that contribute to the atmosphere are wood doors, casings, and crown moldings. Hand-rubbed bronze hardware, column covers, stair structure, sinks, faucets, cabinet pulls (custom cast with the Gulf logo) and signage were created to look like hand-forged metal.

Special attention was given to providing enough light for work stations but still highlighting the collection, which includes traditional Plains Native American clothing, spurs, saddles, chaps, pottery, firearms, and paintings from the era of the Old West.

The 50th floor is designed as conference space, while the floor below houses offices. Furnishings throughout are Western or Southwestern in style, including Spanish Colonial antiques, and are fabricated in leather, wood, or bronze. Soft seating areas throughout all three floors create informal conference areas. Table and floor lamps and Western-style pendant lamps provide an intimate lighting level.

The openness of the office space on the 49th floor accentuates the dramatic curve of the building's north curtainwall, which acts as a skylight above its workstations. A stairway between the 49th and 50th floors opens up the gallery space, increasing interior daylighting and linking the two floors directly. The stair is made of steel with a custom bronze patina that matches the hand-forged bronze look found throughout the project. The handrail and guardrail are made of steel tubing wrapped in leather with a saddle-stitching detail. The stair has open risers and wood plank treads.

Doors, casings, crown, and flooring for the 48th and 49th floors were milled from large pine timbers taken from turn-of-the-century industrial buildings. The 50th floor features mahogany doors, casings, and crown; its oak floors were stained to match and accentuate the mahogany. The stairway provides a transition from the formal finishes of the top floor and its conference reception area to the informal offices and finishes below.

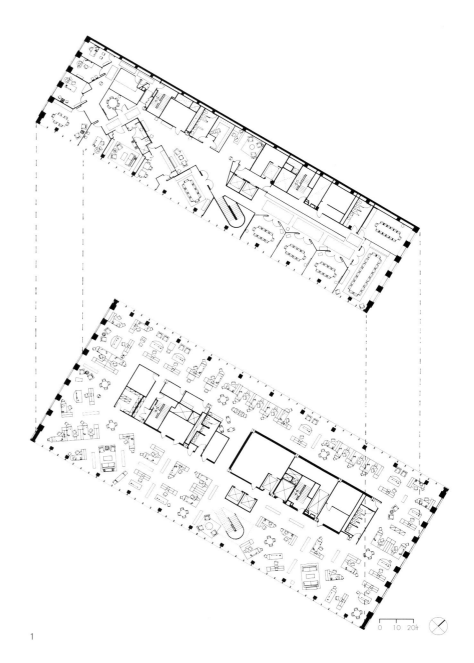

1

2

3

4

5

1   Floor plans for the 49th and 50th floors
2   Collection includes textiles, pottery and other artifacts.
3   Intimate seating areas are arranged throughout the office.
4   Mural faces work stations.
5   Corporate collection includes antique firearms.

Design

The Birdhouse Project 1998

1998
Birdhouse
The Birdhouse Project Executive Committee
Aluminum, acrylic, steel, maple (base)

1

Every two years, the Birdhouse Project of Japan invites the world's leading designers to submit their ideas of what would make the perfect birdhouse. It sends the birdhouses on a traveling exhibit, and publishes a book of the designs along with interviews of their creators. Curt Fentress was invited to participate in the 1998 publication, which featured designs by other noted airport architects including Sir Norman Foster, Renzo Piano, Tadao Ando, Kisho Kurokawa, and Daniel Libeskind.

As with all his designs, Fentress directed his attention to place, purpose, and "person" (in this case, "birds"), in order to insure that the resulting structure would suit its site and region, and would be comfortable and accessible to those living and working in and around it.

Fentress sought to develop a form that evokes an image of nature's quintessential bird shelter: the tree. As a birdhouse, the tree fulfills many basic requirements. At the tree's core is a network of limbs and boughs—the ideal forms to cradle and protect the fragile, interwoven twigs that make up a nest. Elevated from the ground, it protects its denizens from predators below, and its sheltering canopy of leaves offers protection from the elements while allowing sunlight and warm breezes to pass through. It is also an organically complex form that, on a very primitive and emotional level, comforts the soul and reconnects one with the natural environment. Its spreading branches are ideal perches from which a bird can keep watch, perform courtship rituals, bear its young and teach them to fly, or simply enjoy the company of other birds. From a human point of view, there are also the sensory pleasures of dappled light, rustling leaves, and the inexplicable beauty of form and color.

The design uses a single, simple building module, the hyperbolic paraboloid form, because it is a tensile structure that recurs in the firm's airport work, and because its double-curve form suggests a pair of wings in flight. Built from a series of straight elements assembled to form a curve, it is similar to the birds' organic nest forms, created from straight twigs, sticks and other found material. Relative to the amount of material used, such a form also has great strength and stability, recalling again the way in which a bird efficiently uses material to build its home. Manipulation of this single, deceptively simple unit enabled Fentress to create a rich and complex structure.

In Fentress' design, each paraboloid form is a kind of saddle. At the nest's core, the saddles are organized in a simple, structured form that starts out dense at the bottom, and thins out near the top. Places to nest are formed by the joining of saddles side by side, offering a variety of different-sized roosts. The density of the saddles gives the overall structure its strength and resilience. At the outermost layer, the saddles perform a completely different function. Joined only at two of the vertices per module, they become an exhilarating, light-hearted evocation of a canopy of leaves.

1 Curt Fentress' birdhouse design against a sand dune near Perth, Australia
2 Curt Fentress' birdhouse design against a rock wall in Australia
3 Interior geometric shapes are revealed in computer diagram.
4 Birdhouse with birds in nest
5 Computer rendering shows inner alignment of "saddles".

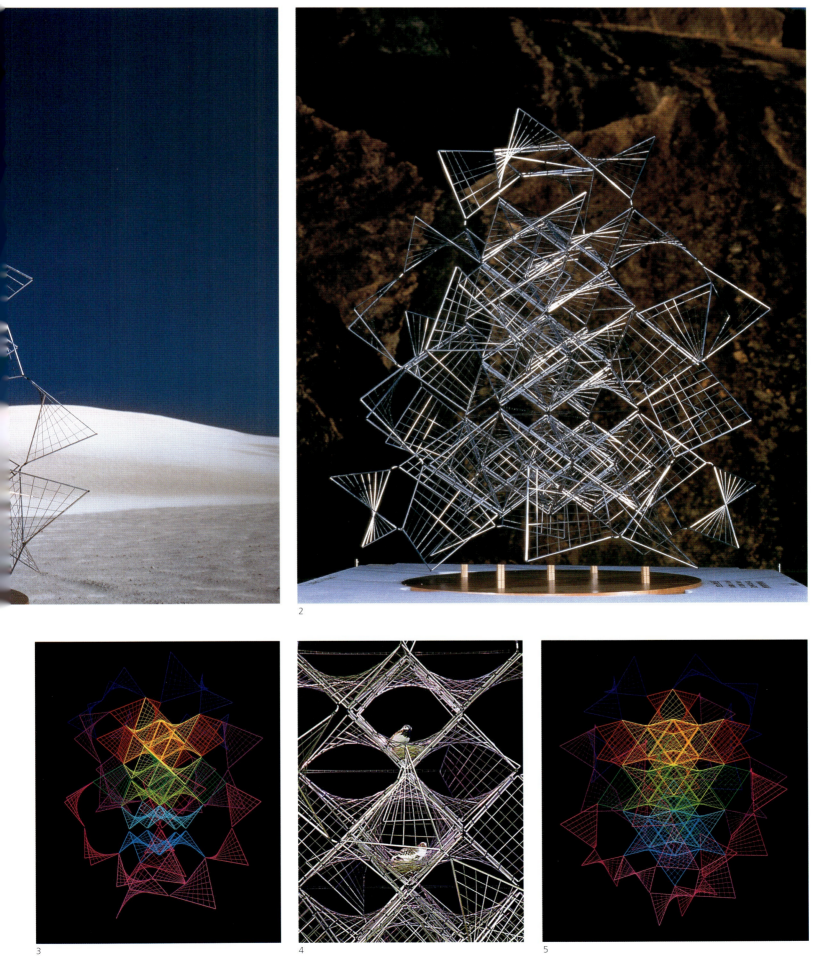

The Birdhouse Project 1998

ICE Terminal Köln-Deutz/Messe (Cologne Convention Center Train Station)

1999
Cologne, Germany
Deutsche Bahn
Transportation/mixed-use development
2 million square feet/185,800 square meters
Concrete, steel, glass
Region: Germany
Context: urban structures from very different historic periods

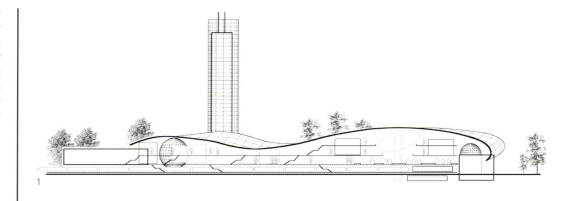

After Fentress Bradburn Architects won an honorable mention in the design competition for expansion of Vienna International Airport in early 1999, the firm was invited to participate with architects from all over the world in a competition to design the ICE Terminal Köln-Deutz/Messe in Cologne, Germany.

The project is a large, mixed-use development of the area on the eastern bank of the Rhine River, serving the city of Cologne. The Cologne Convention Center (Köln-Deutz/Messe) is bounded on the west by local train tracks and the Rhine River, and on the south by train tracks for the high-speed (ICE) trains which come through the main train station on the western side of the river. These tracks converge on the building site in a rudimentary train station which inadvertently cuts off access to the convention center from the city of Cologne, making it accessible only by way of the train station.

One of the goals of the proposed design project was to solve this dilemma, as well as to enhance access to the convention center from the Frankfurt airport, and thereby create a new image for visitors to the city. In addition to train platforms and other supporting structures, the new design was to include a 75,000-square-meter hotel; a retail center and entertainment complex for travelers; an office park with more than 100,000 square meters of generic office space; and registration areas and administrative offices for the convention center.

Not laid out on a Cartesian grid, Old World cities such as Cologne show the layering of history, as generation upon generation have built into the city. Fentress Bradburn's design captures that layering in a modernized, technologically enhanced update by creating a transparent structure which allows one to see the multitude of uses interwoven within a single meta-structure.

The theme of the firm's presentation was *Alles unter einem Dach* ("Everything Under One Roof"), most potently evoked by the mesh which covers the entire complex—a transparent cable-net structure of steel and glass. The firm's design consolidated many of the required features within a single structure. It massed the hotel into a single 30-story tower, united all train platforms in one place, connected the train station to the convention center, and also linked it with the administrative offices and entertainment complex. In order to allow for shared uses with the city, the office park was kept close but separate.

The fluid, curvilinear shape of the building refers to the nearby waters of the Rhine River and echoes the curve of train tracks as they come from different directions and converge within the building. The complex features a large open atrium which brings daylight down into the platform areas on two different levels, thus providing travelers with natural light as they pass through the station. A large purple egg shape occupying the corner of the building serves as a brightly colored beacon at the end of the pedestrian bridge over the Rhine, a feature designed to guide convention-goers coming from the main train station. This bold gesture is used to create a point of arrival, to intrigue arriving passengers and the building's onlookers, and to invest the site with landmark qualities.

3

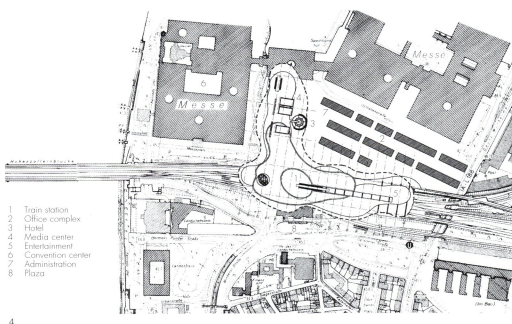

1 Train station
2 Office complex
3 Hotel
4 Media center
5 Entertainment
6 Convention center
7 Administration
8 Plaza

4

1 Section, west façade
2 Model of site, aerial view
3 Model of site, from the southwest
4 Site plan

ICE Terminal Köln-Deutz/Messe **205**

Sacramento High Rise Lot A

Design 2000
Sacramento, California
Westfield-Taylor Lot A Partners, LLC
Office tower and hotel
750,000 square feet/69,675 square meters
spec office space
Glass, steel, granite
Region: agricultural area in California
Context: downtown Sacramento

The site for this office tower in Sacramento is located along Mall A, the civic mall which lies on axis with the California State Capitol and runs perpendicular to the Sacramento River. The building is planned to sit within a few blocks of the Capitol complex. The aim was to re-energize the area with a hinge block development that would connect the area's office district on one side of the mall with a bus station and a refurbished retail center on the other side. Occupants of the office building were anticipated to be mostly those engaged in political or state government work.

The Fentress Bradburn design began with a focus on plant forms and organic shapes, in reference to cultivation in the region. As a synthesis combining these images and the vertical orientation of a standard skyscraper, the tower takes a sinuous, candle-like shape that could serve as a beacon to those approaching Sacramento, providing the city with a progressive image.

The tower is sited close to the civic mall as a strong vertical form that draws the eye. The boutique hotel called for in the plan would sit at the back of the site, facing the retail center. The tower features extensive retail at ground level, with parking facilities low in the building, and office space above.

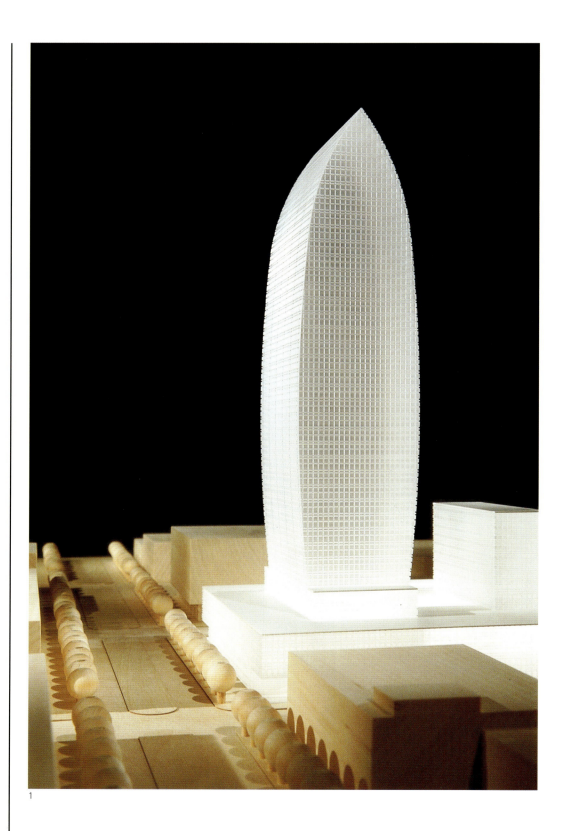

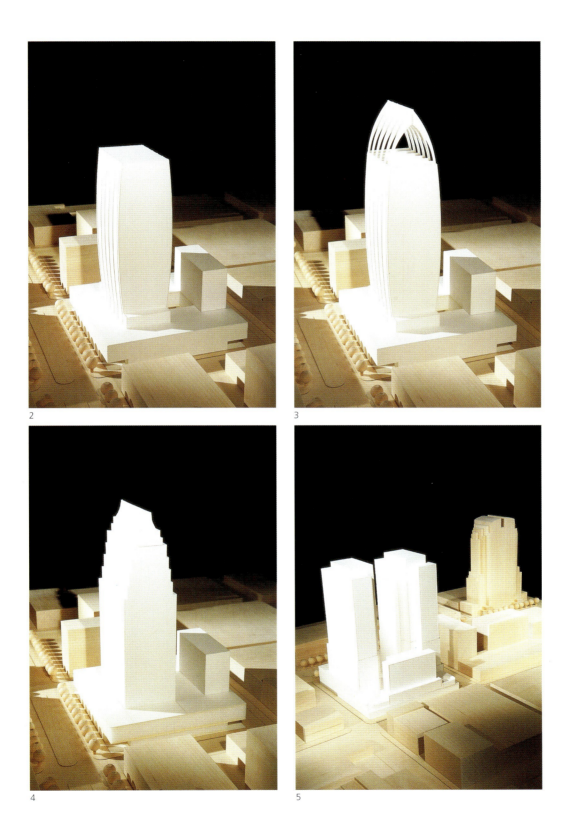

1 Final design concept rises in a candle shape.
2 Design progression: bulge in sides and truncated top
3 Decorative arcade at top
4 Stepped sides approaching pinnacle
5 Multiple-buildings on site

Sacramento High Rise Lot A

Terminal 2, Flughafen München
(Second Terminal, Munich Airport)

1998
Munich, Germany
Airport passenger terminal
2,136,467 square feet/198,536 square meters
25 attached aircraft gates/25 remote aircraft positions, 15 million passengers annually
Concrete, steel and glass
Region: Germany
Context: existing airport

Fentress Bradburn was one of 15 architectural firms invited to submit a design for Terminal 2 of the Munich Airport in Germany, in an international design competition. The new structure, which is slated to be operational by 2005, will handle 15 million air passengers annually.

Fentress Bradburn organized its design around a central terminal, or Great Hall, with an attached linear concourse. At the core of the design is a desire to bring as much daylight as possible into the structure by roofing the terminal with glass. This horizontal glazing lies over an articulated steel skeleton that is shaped in a gentle, aerodynamic waveform. A mechanical system of louvers would protect passengers from the sun but still maintain the high amount of day-lighting, giving travelers direct views of the sky. The openness of the lower floors would allow daylight to penetrate into the deepest levels of the building, making all of the facility's spaces light and airy.

This volume of light also allowed the architects to bring nature indoors in the form of interior courtyards—gardens in both public areas and office spaces, an amenity for all users of the facility. These courtyards also serve to distinguish the landside from the airside of the terminal.

This simple, easily understood airport terminal addresses passenger convenience and comfort by locating retail and concessions at all stages of the travel process, so that travelers never have to venture off the path to their gates in order to shop or eat.

Fentress Bradburn's design also succeeds in blending the new structure with existing architecture, as the glass roof's low sweeping curve meets the soaring space of the Munich Airport Center in a respectful, rather than competitive, gesture.

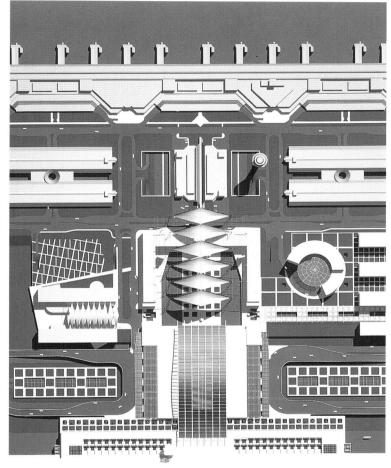
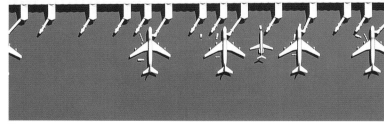

1　Computer rendering, main façade at approach road
2　Juncture of new terminal with existing structure at back
3　Model of site
4　Computer rendering, view from tarmac

Terminal 2, Flughafen München

5 Computer rendering, interior of Great Hall
6 Computer rendering, interior near juncture with existing terminal
7 Section, side façade
8 Section, front façade
9 Site plan

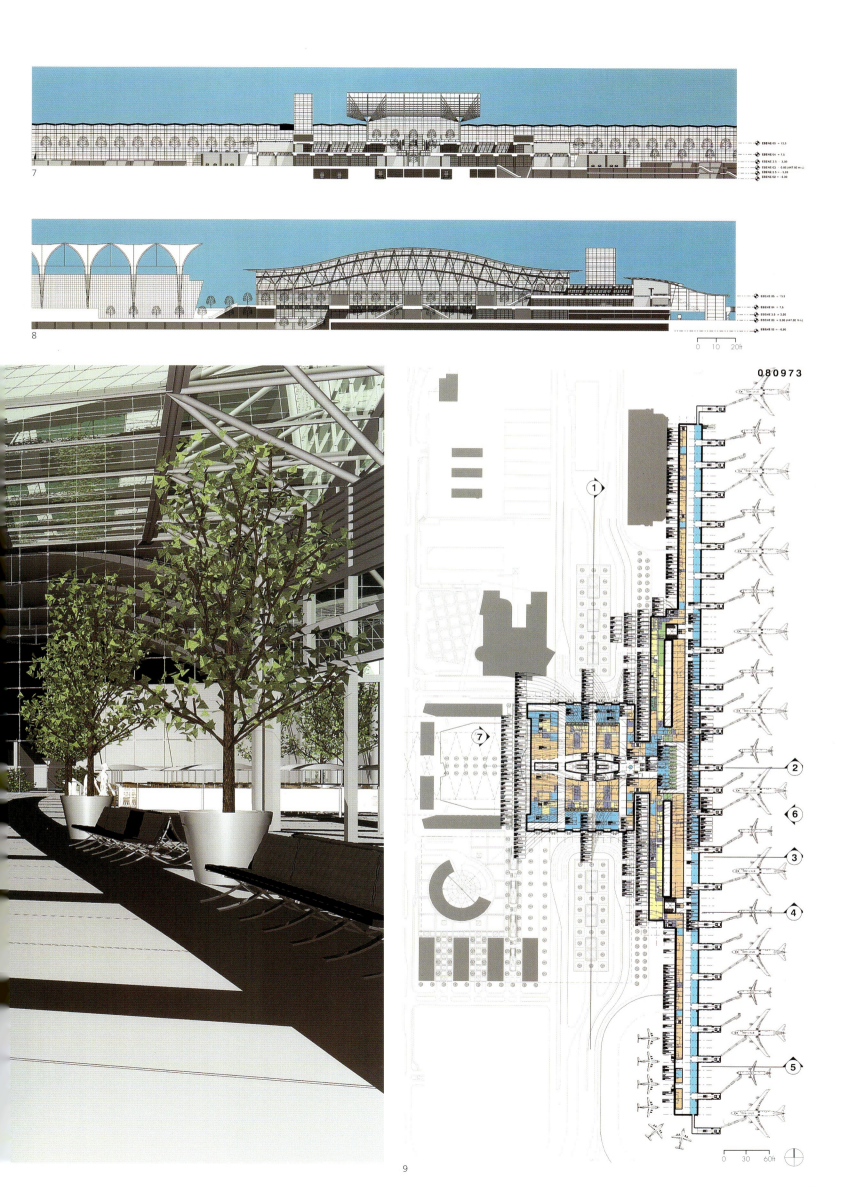

Terminal 2, Flughafen München 211

Dinosaur Discovery Museum

1992
Cañon City, Colorado
Museum
Region: western United States
Context: semi-arid desert
Guiding metaphor: discovery

Like the skeleton of a felled prehistoric beast, the visible exterior structure of the Dinosaur Discovery Museum disappears into the earth, hinting at the unseen. In this way, Fentress Bradburn's design celebrates the found objects of palaeontology as well as the methods by which those objects are found.

Visitors descend down a broad walkway into the earth at the southeast end of the site in order to enter the museum. The reception and first gallery areas are lit from above by a long row of large rectangular skylights. Passing through this area and ascending to the second floor, one finds a series of stylized ribs soaring overhead. These form a glassed-in canopy for on-grade exhibits. The scale and deployment of the ribs, which are grounded in the first-floor skylights, play to the imagination, giving visitors a vivid sense of being inside a dinosaur. Topographic features of the site, such as a shallow canyon which cuts through it, and a natural terrace on-grade with the museum's first level, offer visitors spectacular views of their surroundings.

In 1996, Fentress Bradburn earned an award of distinction for its design of the Dinosaur Discovery Museum from the Denver chapter of the American Institute of Architects.

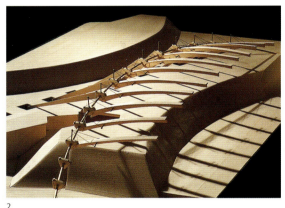

1 Initial sketch
2 Model, from northeast, showing ribs over terrace
3 Model, from north, showing ribs anchored in rectangular skylights
4 Ribs follow topography of site, sinking into shallow canyon.
5 Model, from southeast
6 Line drawing
7 Rendering, showing entrance at lower right

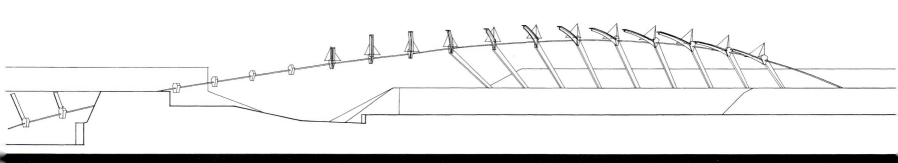

Colorado History Museum Expansion

2000
Denver, Colorado
Museum
Colorado Historical Society
Sandstone, steel, glass
Region: western United States
Context: museum plaza
Guiding metaphor: Colorado geography

Fentress Bradburn began the design process for the Colorado History Museum expansion with a geometric form: a glass box that references the building's original geometric design and showcases the colorful mural at the front of the building.

As the site was examined, this concept was superseded by a more sculptural form, whose massing would complement the original museum. Edgy shapes were used to portray the adventurousness and risk-taking nature of those who explored and finally settled the diverse geography of Colorado. The shape became tectonic, referencing the thrust of mountain forms and emphasizing their angularity. The architects also experimented with a more fluid version, in tune with river imagery. The final design greets the user with a visceral narrative that speaks through the abstracted landforms of the river, the range, the summit, and the Flatirons.

The Flatirons are an upthrust sandstone strata that grace the Front Range of the Rocky Mountains, a dramatic shape at the junction of mountain and plain. This is realized in the building as a closed, jutting form that would serve as the museum's street presence. The river carves the building into two forms, opening the interior to include the sky through a narrow glass atrium and, in the process, creating a canyon-like interior exhibit gallery. The range is typified in a more horizontal element toward the back of the building. The summit serves as the museum's beckoning point, a squared-off pinnacle thrust around the side and over the top of the existing museum to establish the addition's presence and personality for observers from Civic Center Park.

1

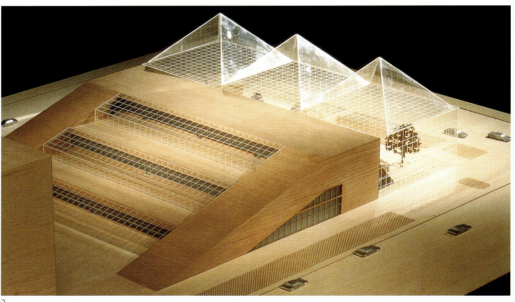

2

The texture of the exterior is created using native stone in irregular configurations in order to simulate patterns in nature. Entrance into the museum is from a plaza between the old and new buildings, supplanting the former entrance and helping the addition maintain a solid rock-wall presence along Thirteenth Avenue. The two buildings remain separate above grade, linked by below-grade exhibit halls. Descent into that area gives visitors a mining-like experience consonant with another part of Colorado's geography and history. The new space includes exhibit halls and galleries as well as office space, a library, and an auditorium.

1   Computer rendering of glass façade and people
2   Northwest façade, showing glass pyramids at top
3   Early design following tectonic approach
4   River concept
5   Sketch, showing proximity of existing structure (left) and expansion (right)
6   Final design, west façade
7   Model showing proximity of two buildings, from northwest

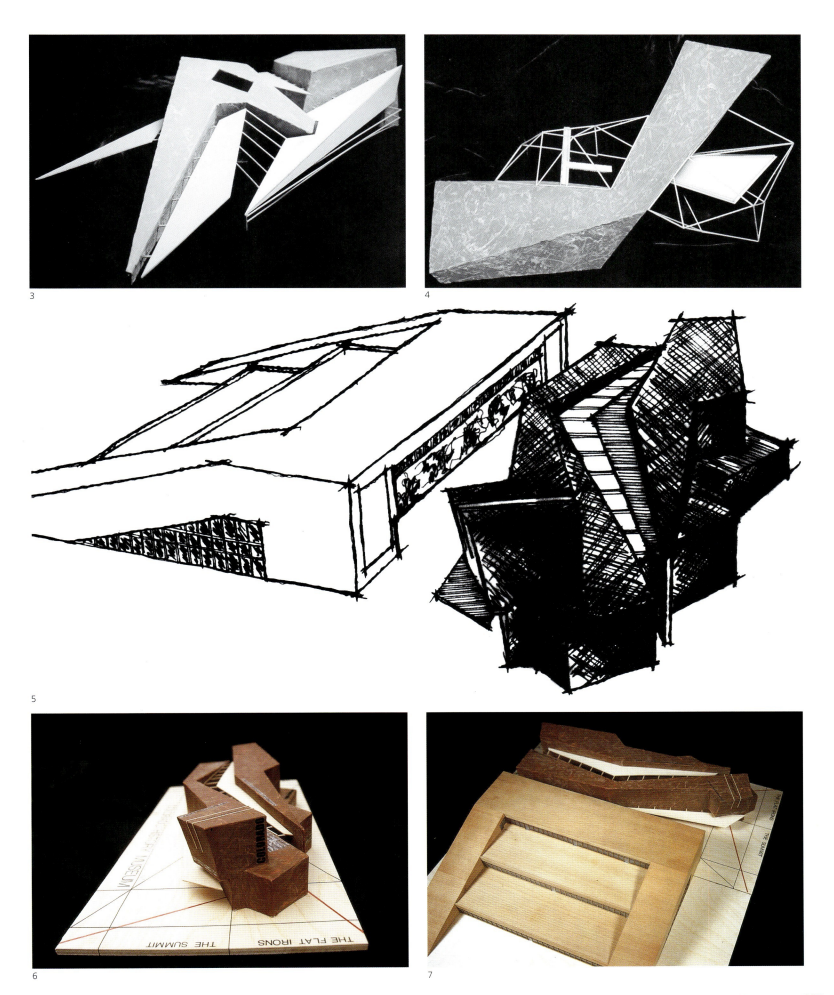

Colorado History Museum Expansion 215

Central California History Museum

1999
Fresno, California
Fresno City and County Historical Society
45,591 square feet/4,235 square meters
Cast-in-place concrete, precast concrete, steel, glass, drywall and wood trim interiors

1

2

Since the introduction of water into the Central Valley has literally sustained life there, Fentress Bradburn turned to forms of water flow, control, and storage for dramatic metaphors to organize its entry in the 1999 design competition for the Central California History Museum. These are realized in three forms: the water tower, the dam, and the reservoir.

Tower
The firm's design of the museum greets the visitor with an abstracted tower form which serves as the primary vertical circulation hub for the building. Enclosed in transparent glass walls, the elevators, like water, have a shimmering quality as their motion within the tower is subtly revealed.

Dam
Between the lobby atrium and the exhibit spaces stands a dam-like wall, curved and sloped, three stories high, and made of cast-in-place concrete. This is the boundary between lobby and exhibit space, openly marked by a narrow glass skylight along its edge. Pedestrian walkways are suspended between the elevator tower and the dam wall, traversing the open space of the three-story-high lobby. A spillway-like water feature runs down the sloped face of the dam wall, across the lobby floor and into a reflecting pool at the tower.

Reservoir
The exhibits and curatorial space are the museum's reservoir of the Central Valley's heritage. This portion of the building is clad in architectural precast panels. The heavy, ordered look of these walls stands in sharp contrast to the more spontaneous forms of the lobby.

The first level of the museum is taken up with retail and administrative spaces, leaving the second and third levels for exhibits. Visitors begin at a dense collage of local images and artifacts, then proceed into three interconnected zones, each with its own theme. The first focuses on the valley before human habitation, the second on those who settled the valley, the third on the introduction of water into the environment.

At the center of the second level's exhibition space is the most dramatic element of the design: a 50-foot-high cylindrical wall which protrudes above roof level, hangs down into the two-story-high space, and is topped by a flat skylight. Arranged on both the inner and outer curved surfaces of the Culture Dome, as it is termed, are images and artifacts of all peoples who have inhabited the area, making this striking feature a paean to the Central Valley's cultural diversity.

The museum site spans an entire city block in Fresno, but the museum building itself takes up only the southeast corner. Fentress Bradburn's master plan would keep the site's existing farmer's market, devoting the northeast corner to it, and create a central pedestrian spine that would feature outdoor interactive interpretive exhibits on Central Valley features outside Fresno. The remainder of the site would be devoted to a community garden, a theater, a café, and a bookstore.

1 Presentation board with site plan
2 West façade of museum with tower atrium at right
3 Night-time computer rendering of tower and atrium
4 Inspiration/sketch boards

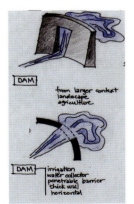
DAM — from larger context
landscape
agriculture

DAM — irrigation
water collector
penetrable barrier
thick wall
horizontal

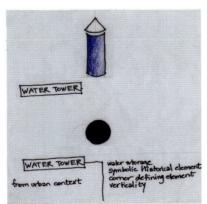
WATER TOWER — from urban context
water storage
symbolic historical element
corner defining element
verticality

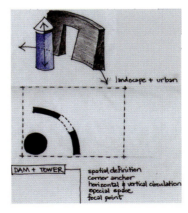
DAM + TOWER — landscape + urban
spatial definition
corner anchor
horizontal & vertical circulation
special space
focal point

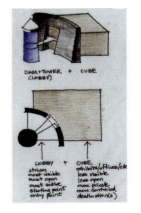
DAM + TOWER + CUBE (LOBBY)
LOBBY — atrium
most visible
most active
starting point
entry point

CUBE — exhibits/offices/etc
less visible
more private
more controlled
destination(s)

Central California History Museum 217

5

6

7

Third Floor Plan
Scale 1/16"=1'-0"

		Program	Actual
1	Elevator Lobby		
2	Board Room	700	691
3	General Office	1,000	1,052
4	Toilets	120	124
5	Janitor / Storage	120	96
6	Staff Room / Kitchen	120	109
7	Copy / Supply	200	202
8	Education Office	150	150
9	Business Office	150	150
10	Public Information	150	150
11	Director's Office	350	351
12	Development Office	150	150
13	Volunteer Work Room	150	150
14	Conference / Library	225	225
15	Storage	200	195
16	Exhibit Work Rooms	500	500
17	Temporary Gallery	3,000	3,075
18	Bridge		
19	Mechanical		
20	Culture Dome		

Second Floor Plan
Scale 1/16"=1'-0"

		Program	Actual
1	Elevator Lobby		
2	Resource Room	1,000	1,002
3	Orientation Theater	500	623
4	Exhibit Introduction	2,000	2,151
5	Core Exhibits	6,000	5,974
6	Mechanical		

Ground Floor Plan
Scale 1/16"=1'-0"

		Program	Actual
1	Vestibule	300	296
2	Lobby	2,000	2,394
3	Reception		
4	Security	150	158
5	Gift Shop	1,000	1,014
6	Multifunction	2,100	2,082
7	Toilets	700	519
8	Gift Shop Storage	200	216
9	Gift Shop Office	250	250
10	Catering Kitchen	200	198
11	Ed./Program Storage	200	200
12	Equip./Ed. Materials	200	198
13	Mechanical		
14	Shipping / Receiving	400	399
15	Loading / Delivery		
16	Public Garden		
17	Private Garden		
18	Reflecting Pool		
19	Fountain		
20	Drop-off		
21	Bus Loading		

Basement Plan
Scale 1/16"=1'-0"

		Program	Actual
1	Archive Storage	2,000	2,006
2	Collection Storage	5,000	5,008
3	Workroom	300	252
4	Conservation / Work	300	305
5	Registration	250	256
6	Documentation	50	54
7	Electrical		
8	Mechanical		
9	Temporary Storage	300	290

Total Areas

Zone		Program	Actual
A	Public/Noncollection	6,650	7,086
B	Public/Collection	12,000	12,202
C	Nonpublic/Noncoll.	5,365	5,357
D	Nonpublic/Collect.	8,550	8,570
total net		32,565	33,215
total gross		45,591	47,429
factor		1.40	1.43

8

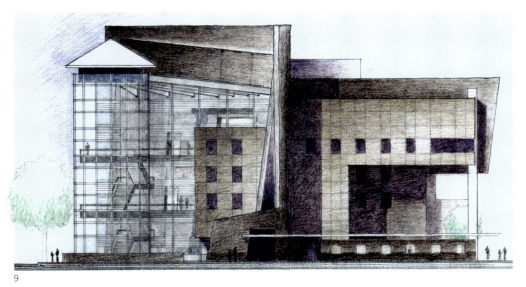

9

12

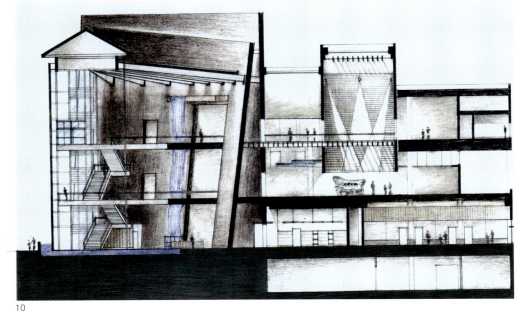

10

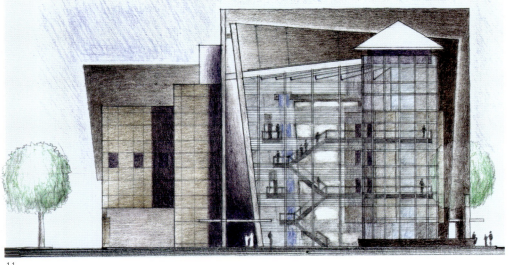

11

5   Model, showing tower and atrium
6   Model, from above, showing curve of "dam"
7   Aerial shot of site model, from the southwest
8   Presentation boards
9   Elevation, south façade, showing glassed-in atrium
10 Culture Dome cuts through top two floors at right.
11 Elevation, west façade, showing glassed-in atrium
12 Computer rendering, interior of atrium

Colorado Christian University

1999
Lakewood, Colorado
University campus
Colorado Christian University
280 acres (site), 800,000 square feet/
74,320 square meters (buildings)
Sandstone, brick, precast concrete
Region: western United States
Context: foothills of the Rocky Mountains

1

2

Having outgrown its original facilities, Colorado Christian University acquired a scenic, undeveloped, 280-acre site in the foothills of the Rocky Mountains just southwest of Denver, to which it plans to move all of its facilities. Invited by university officials to submit an entry in the design competition for the campus, Fentress Bradburn created a master plan that is a testament both to the mission of the university and to the works of God as seen in the natural beauty of the new site's mountain valley.

The design is scaled to accommodate 3,000 students on a campus with 800,000 square feet of building space, including a chapel, library, administration building, alumni and visitor center, faculty offices, a graduate studies facility, a student center, a dining facility, residence halls, and schools of theology, music, humanities, education and business, as well as athletic facilities.

The site is bounded by roads north and south; to the west by Lyons Ridge, a granite-and-sandstone formation covered with scrub oak, pine, and mountain mahogany; and to the east by a towering ridge of red sandstone called, because of its shape, the Hog Back. The firm's design proposes an entrance to the site from the north, with the greater part of the campus in a tranquil setting at the lower part of the valley, leaving a soccer stadium, baseball fields, and swimming facilities tucked into the mountain landscape in the upper meadow.

Entry to the site is from a nearby state highway. Visitors are given a brief glimpse of the campus before being guided through a wooded area and emerging into the valley. The campus' first dramatic impression is rendered by its chapel, the iconic presence of the campus and its most important symbolic building. One sees instantly the crystalline upper portion of the church—glass on a highly articulated wood frame—representing heavenly aspirations. At its base, the structure's low ashlar-stone walls are grounded in a rough form of rubble stone, a reference to the earthly context of existence.

In front of the chapel, the design creates a large public gathering place, with another such public square set before the university library. A pedestrian spine spanning the entire village links these two large open areas with smaller ones—plazas, cloisters, courtyards, and gardens. This variety of size in the campus' public spaces creates venues for gatherings of all kinds, from individual discipleship between faculty and students, to large-scale events, always preserving the human scale of the campus.

A series of arcades and colonnades along this spine provides shelter from the elements and helps unify the university grounds. Layout of the village itself is organized around planning grids that shift in relation to the topographic constraints of the valley floor. Parking is kept to the perimeter of the village in order to maintain the campus' pedestrian character.

1 Rendering of site, from northwest, with chapel at middle left
2 Rendering superimposed on aerial photograph of site
3 Site model, showing athletic fields at top of valley

Colorado Christian University

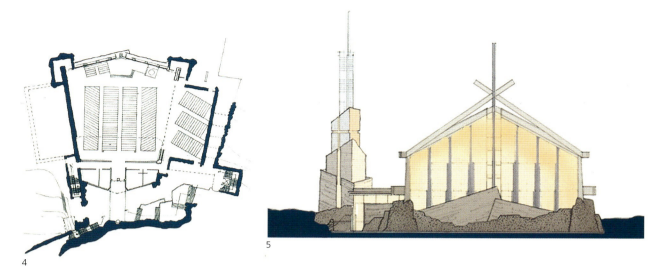

4

5

6

7

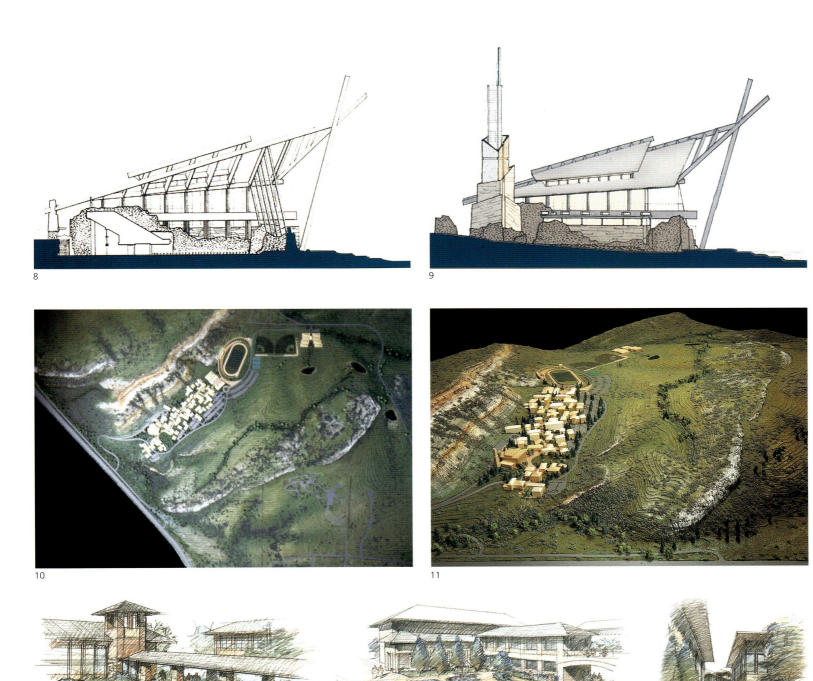

4   Floor plan, chapel
5   Elevation, chapel
6   Model of chapel from above
7   Rendering of chapel
8   Elevation
9   Elevation with bell tower
10 Site model from above
11 Model from north end of site
12 Rendering, arcade
13 Rendering, residence hall
14 Rendering, pedestrian spine of campus

Colorado Christian University

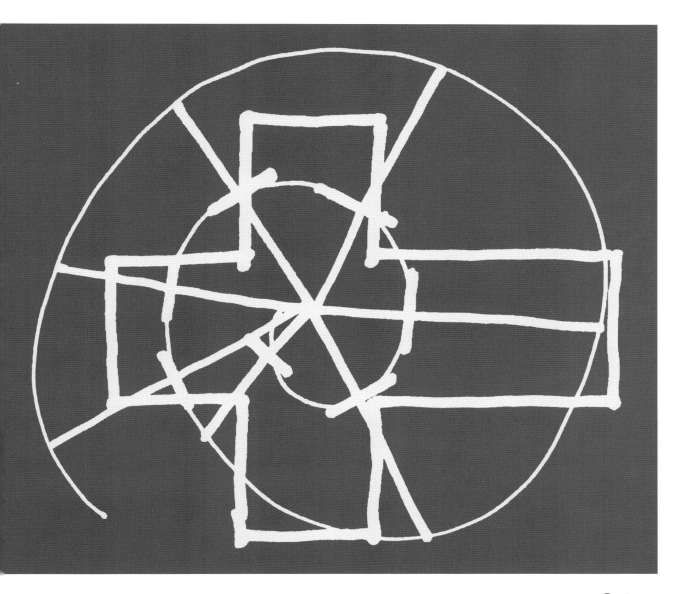

Firm Profile

Associates and Collaborators

Principals
Curtis W. Fentress, FAIA, RIBA
James H. Bradburn, FAIA
Ronald R. Booth, AIA
Michael O. Winters, AIA
Thomas J. Walsh, AIA
Brian H. Chaffee, AIA

Associate Principals
John M. Kudrycki
Jack M. Mousseau, AIA
Ned S. Kirschbaum, AIA
Jeffrey W. Olson

Senior Associates
Mark A. Wagner
Gregory R. Gidez
Robert M. Louden
Todd R. Britton
Karen Gilbert

Associates
Jayne A. Coburn
Thomas P. Theobald
John C. Wurzenberger Jr.
Mark A. Outman
Catherine H. Dunn
Greg Billingham
Jack Cook

Collaborators
Peter Akins
Scott Allen
Robin Ault
Amanda Bonsante
Stormy Brettmann
Rexford Canady
Geoffrey Cerilli
Garrett Christnacht
Jonathan Coppin
Christina Cortright
Daniel Culross
Marc Dietrick
Tina Du Mond
Rafael Espinoza
Delia Esquivel
Antonio Gomez
Carlton Goodiel
Deborah Goodiel
Trisha Healy
Brandi Hill
Lisa Hillmer
Sandra Hunter-Debnam
Kristen Hurty
Nathan James
Charles Johns
Loree Karr
Kristoffer Kenton
Jason Loui
Natalie Lucero
Deborah Lucking
Mike Miller
Irina Mokrova
Val Moses
Melissa Parker
Christian Peters
Theresa Peters
Felipe Pineiro
Cory Poole
Nejeebkhan Rayammarakk
Renae Richards
Robert Riffel
Mike Rinken
Jorge Rodriguez
Susan Rossberg
Tymmie Serr
Valerie Slack
James Sobey
Amy Solomon
Joseph Solomon
Derek Starkenburg
Leslie Stuart
Richard Talley
Alexa Taylor
Alex Thome
Tanya Troiano
Denise Trujillo
Elizabeth Turner
Shawn Turney
Marilyn White
Sonny Willier
Jacqueline Wisniewski
Bradly Wonnacott

Selected Competitions

1998
Civic Center Parking Structure, Fort Collins, Colorado (1st prize)

1997
3993 Howard Hughes Parkway Office Building, Las Vegas, Nevada (1st prize)

1996
The New Doha International Airport, Doha, Qatar (1st prize)
The AEC Design Competition 1996, Long Beach, California (1st prize)
Larimer County Justice Center, Fort Collins, Colorado (1st prize)

1995
Hughes Center Office Tower, Las Vegas, Nevada (1st prize)
City of Oakland Administration Buildings, Oakland, California (1st prize)

1994
New Inchon Metropolitan Airport Terminal, Seoul, Korea (1st prize)

1992
National Cowboy Hall of Fame expansion and renovation, Oklahoma City, Oklahoma (1st prize)
Clark County Government Center, Las Vegas, Nevada (1st prize)

1991
National Museum of Wildlife Art, Jackson, Wyoming (1st prize)

1989
Natural Resources Building, Olympia, Washington (1st prize)

1987
Colorado Convention Center, Denver, Colorado (1st prize)

1986
Data General Field Engineering Logistics Center, Fountain, Colorado (1st prize)

Selected Awards

Firm Awards

Firm of the Year
1996 Western Mountain Region of the American Institute of Architects

Firm of the Year
1994 Colorado Chapter of the American Institute of Architects

Selected Project Awards

1999 Broadway
1990 Merit Award, American Institute of Architects, Colorado Chapter
1985 Honor Award, American Institute of Architects, Western Mountain Region

Black American West Museum
1991 Merit Award, American Institute of Architects, Western Mountain Region
1991 Merit Award, American Institute of Architects, Denver Chapter
1988 Stephen H. Hart Historic Preservation Award, Colorado Historical Society

City of Oakland Administration Buildings
1999 Design–Build Excellence Award, Design-Build Institute of America

Clark County Government Center
1998 Honor Award, American Institute of Architects, Colorado Chapter
1998 Honor Award, National Association of Industrial and Office Properties (NAIOP)
1997 Honor Award, American Institute of Architects, Western Mountain Region
1996 Grand Award, Gold Nugget Award, Pacific Coast Builders Conference and *Builder* magazine

Colorado Convention Center
1991 Engineering Excellence, Consulting Engineers Council
1991 Honor Award, American Institute of Architects, Denver Chapter
1990 Honor Award, American Institute of Architects, Colorado Chapter
1990 Merit Award, American Institute of Architects, Western Mountain Region

Dinosaur Discovery Museum
1996 Award of Distinction, American Institute of Architects, Denver Chapter

Denver International Airport Passenger Terminal Complex
1995 Honor Award, Design for Transportation, U.S. Department of Transportation
1994 Honor Award, American Institute of Architects, Colorado Chapter
1994 Honor Award, American Institute of Architects, Western Mountain Region
1994 Honor Award, American Institute of Architects, Denver Chapter
1993 Excellence Award, Consulting Engineering Council of Colorado
1993 Excellence Award, New York Association of Consulting Engineers

Jefferson County Human Services Building
1991 Honor Award, American Institute of Architects, Western Mountain Region
1991 Merit Award, American Institute of Architects, Denver Chapter

Museum of Western Art/The Navarre
1987 Honor Award, American Institute of Architects, Denver Chapter
1985 Excellence in Design, Honor Award, American Institute of Architects, Western Mountain Region

1985 Honor Award, Excellence in Historic Preservation, American Institute of Architects, Denver Chapter
1985 Certificate of Excellence, American Architecture Awards
1985 Honor Award "Best of Show," American Institute of Architects, Denver Chapter
1984 Award of Honor, Downtown Denver, Inc., Quality of Life Awards
1984 Annual Design Awards, American Society of Interior Designers
1984 Design Award, American Institute of Architects, Colorado Chapter

National Museum of Wildlife Art
1996 Honor Award, American Institute of Architects, Denver Chapter
1996 Award of Distinction People's Choice Award, Denver AIA
1996 Honorable Mention, American Institute of Architects, Colorado Chapter
1996 Honor Award, American Institute of Architects, Western Mountain Region Chapter
1995 Grand Award, Gold Nugget Awards, Pacific Coast Builders Conference
1995 Award of Distinction People's Choice Award, Denver AIA

Natural Resources Building
1997 Design-Build Excellence Award, Design Build Institute of America
1996 Merit Award, American Institute of Architects, Colorado Chapter
1993 Award of Merit, Architecture and Energy, American Institute of Architects, Portland Chapter

Peery's Egyptian Theater
1999 Citation Award, American Institute of Architects, Colorado Chapter
1999 Honor Award, American Institute of Architects, Western Mountain Region
1998 Honor Award, American Institute of Architects, Denver Chapter
1998 Merit Award, United States Institute for Theatre Technology
1997 Award of Honor, National Preservation Honor Awards, National Trust for Historic Preservation, 1997
1997 Merit Award, United States Institute for Theatre Technology

Ronstadt Transit Center
1991 Merit Award, American Institute of Architects, Western Mountain Region
1991 Merit Award, American Institute of Architects, Denver Chapter
1991 Design Award, American Institute of Architects, Colorado Chapter

Regional Transportation Commission/Regional Flood Control District Headquarters
2000 Honor Award, American Institute of Architects, Colorado Chapter
1999 Honor Award, American Institute of Architects, Las Vegas Chapter

The Tritch Building
1999 Merit Award, American Institute of Architects, Denver Chapter
1998 Historic Renovation Award, *Building Design & Construction*
1998 Award of Citation, American Institute of Architects, Western Mountain Region
1998 State Honor Award, Colorado Preservation, Inc.

University of Colorado Mathematics Building/Gemmill Engineering Library
1994 Merit Award, American Institute of Architects, Denver Chapter
1993 Steve Dach Award for Excellence in Colorado Masonry, Best Natural Stone Project, Rocky Mountain Masonry Institute
1993 Citation Award, American Association of School Administrators and the American Institute of Architects

Chronological List of Buildings, Projects and Credits

1980

Crystal Center
Design 1980
Denver, Colorado
Chesman Realty Company
Principal in charge of design:
Curtis W. Fentress
Design team: Brian Chaffee, Lisa K. Fudge

One Mile High Plaza
Design 1980
Denver, Colorado
J. Roulier Interests
Principal in charge of design:
Curtis W. Fentress
Design team: Brian Chaffee, Mary Jane Donovan, Lisa K. Fudge, Chris Weber

Terrace Towers Master Plan
Design 1980–86
J. Roulier Interests
Principal in charge of design:
Curtis W. Fentress
Principal in charge of production:
James H. Bradburn
Design team: Robert Busch, Brian Chaffee, Gregory R. Gidez, Stuart A. Schunck, Dave B. Weigand

Terrace Building
Design/Completion 1980/1981
Englewood, Colorado
J. Roulier Interests
Principal in charge of design:
Curtis W. Fentress
Design team: Robert T. Brodie, Brian Chaffee, Mary Jane Donovan, Lisa K. Fudge, Frederic M. Harrington

Southbridge One
Design/Completion 1980/1981
Littleton, Colorado
J. Roulier Interests
Principal in charge of design:
Curtis W. Fentress
Design team: Robert Brodie, Lisa K. Fudge, Elizabeth Hamilton, Frederic M. Harrington, Robert J. O'Donnell

Milestone Tower
Design/Completion 1980/1982
Englewood, Colorado
J. Roulier Interests
Principal in charge of design:
Curtis W. Fentress
Principal in charge of production:
James H. Bradburn
Design team: Benjamin Berg, Donald W. DeCoster, Mary Jane Donovan, Robert C. Grubbs, John L. Mason

Milestone Square Master Plan
Design/Completion 1981/1986
Englewood, Colorado
J. Roulier Interests
Principal in charge of design:
Curtis W. Fentress
Principal in charge of production:
James H. Bradburn
Design team: Robert Busch, Brian Chaffee, Gregory R. Gidez, Stuart A. Schunck, David B. Weigand

Kittredge Building
Design/Completion 1980/1981
Denver, Colorado
Kittredge Properties
Principal in charge of design:
Curtis W. Fentress
Principal in charge of production:
James H. Bradburn
Design team: Deborah R. Allen, Brian Chaffee, Peter Frothingham, Gregory R. Gidez, Frederic M. Harrington, James F. Hartman, JoAnne Hege, Patrick M. McKelvey, Robert J. O'Donnell, John R. Taylor

1981

116 Inverness Drive East
Design/Completion 1981/1982
Englewood, Colorado
Central Development Group
Principal in charge of design:
Curtis W. Fentress
Principal in charge of production:
James H. Bradburn
Design team: Gregory R. Gidez, James F. Hartman, Michael Kicklighter, Dan Naegele, James Niemi, Byron Stewart

1999 Broadway
Design/Completion 1981/1985
Denver, Colorado
First Interstate Structures, Inc.
Principal in charge of design:
Curtis W. Fentress
Principal in charge of production:
James H. Bradburn
Project designer: Michael O. Winters
Project manager: John K. McCauley
Job captain: Brit Probst
Design team: Robert T. Brodie, Robert G. Datson, Donald W. DeCoster, Lawrence Depenbusch, Douglas Dick, Gregory R. Gidez, Frederic M. Harrington, Michael Kicklighter, John M. Kudrycki, John L. Mason, Patrick M. McKelvey, James Niemi, Clement Okoye, Frederick R. Pax, Sandy Prouty, John R. Taylor, Toshika Yoshida

Holy Ghost Roman Catholic Church
Design/Completion 1981/1985
Denver, Colorado
Lawder Corporation
Principal in charge of design:
Curtis W. Fentress
Principal in charge of production:
James H. Bradburn
Project architect: Michael O. Winters
Project manager: John L. Mason
Design team: Elizabeth Hamilton, John M. Kudrycki, Patrick M. McKelvey, Bruce R. Mosteller, John R. Taylor

1982

Reliance Tower
Design 1982
Denver, Colorado
Reliance Development
Principal in charge of design:
Curtis W. Fentress
Principal in charge of production:
James H. Bradburn
Design team: Robert T. Brodie, Brian Chaffee, Gary Chamer, Lisa K. Fudge, Gregory R. Gidez, JoAnne Hege, John K. McCauley, Patrick M. McKelvey, James Niemi, Michael O. Winters

Capitol Tower/J.D. Tower
Design 1982
Denver, Colorado
Dikeou Family Interest
Principal in charge of design:
Curtis W. Fentress
Design collaborator: Gary Chamer

Odd Fellows Hall
Design/Completion 1982/1983
Denver, Colorado
Cambridge Development Group
Principal in charge of design:
Curtis W. Fentress
Principal in charge of production:
James H. Bradburn
Design team: Deborah R. Allen, Frederic M. Harrington, James F. Hartman, JoAnne Hege, Leslie Leydorf, Carla McConnell, Patrick M. McKelvey, James Niemi, Nathaniel A. Taiwo, Dave B. Weigand, Richard T. Weldon, Toshika Yoshida

Museum of Western Art/The Navarre
Design/Completion 1982/1983
Denver, Colorado
William Foxley
Principal in charge of design:
Curtis W. Fentress
Principal in charge of production:
James H. Bradburn
Associate architect: John Prosser
Design team: Deborah R. Allen, Donald W. DeCoster, Douglas Dick

Southbridge Plaza
Design/Completion 1982/1984
Littleton, Colorado
Southbridge Plaza Association, Inc.
Principal in charge of design:
Curtis W. Fentress
Principal in charge of production:
James H. Bradburn
Design team: Elizabeth Hamilton, Kimble Hobbs, Bruce R. Mosteller, W. Harrison Phillips, Brit Probst, Bryon Stewart

Welton Street Parking Garage
Design/Completion 1982/1985
Denver, Colorado
Lawder Corporation
Principal in charge of design:
Curtis W. Fentress
Principal in charge of production:
James H. Bradburn
Project architect: Michael O. Winters
Project manager: John K. McCauley
Job captain: Patrick M. McKelvey
Design team: Douglas Dick, Frederic M. Harrington, Kimble Hobbs, John L. Mason, Brit Probst

1800 Grant Street
Design/Completion 1982/1985
Denver, Colorado
1800 Grant Street Association, Ltd
Principal in charge of design:
Curtis W. Fentress
Principal in charge of production:
James H. Bradburn
Project designer: Brian Chaffee
Project manager: John K. McCauley
Job captain: James F. Hartman
Design team: Deborah R. Allen, Gregory R. Gidez, Renata Hajek, JoAnne Hege, Mark A. Wagner, Toshika Yoshida

1983

YMCA
Design 1983
Denver, Colorado
Jeffrey Selby & Jay Peterson, Associates
Principal in charge of design:
Curtis W. Fentress
Principal in charge of production:
James H. Bradburn
Design collaborator: Gary Chamer

The Balboa Company Corporate Headquarters
Design/Completion 1983/1984
Denver, Colorado
Captiva Corporation
Principal in charge of design:
Curtis W. Fentress
Principal in charge of production:
James H. Bradburn
Design team: Deborah R. Allen, Donald W. DeCoster, Gregory R. Gidez, JoAnne Hege, Stan Kulesa, James W. O'Neill, Toshika Yoshida

Republic Park Hotel
Design/Completion 1983/1985
Englewood, Colorado
Stan Miles Properties
Principal in charge of design:
Curtis W. Fentress
Principal in charge of production:
James H. Bradburn
Project manager: Mark A. Wagner
Interior designer: Victor Huff and Associates
Design team: Lyle R. Anderson, Brian Chaffee, Gary Chamer, John K. McCauley

One DTC
Design/Completion 1983/1985
Englewood, Colorado
Corum Real Estate Interests
Principal in charge of design:
Curtis W. Fentress
Principal in charge of production:
James H. Bradburn
Project designer: B. Edward Balkin
Project manager: Dalas Disney
Design team: Deborah R. Allen, Lyle R. Anderson, Garrett H. Christnacht, Gregory R. Gidez, Renata Hajek, Frederic M. Harrington, Stan Kulesa, James Niemi, Clement Okoye, Brit Probst, John R.Taylor, Toshika Yoshida

Tele-Communications, Inc., Headquarters
(Terrace Tower II)
Design/Completion 1983/1985
Englewood, Colorado
J. Roulier Interests
First Texas Savings Association
Principal in charge of design:
Curtis W. Fentress
Principal in charge of production:
James H. Bradburn
Project designer: Michael O. Winters
Design team: Deborah R. Allen, Donald W. DeCoster, Frank G. Hege, John M. Kudrycki, James Niemi, Frederick R. Pax, Brit Probst

1984

Englewood Mixed-Use Center
Design 1984
Englewood, Colorado
Talley Corporation
Principal in charge of design:
Curtis W. Fentress
Principal in charge of production:
James H. Bradburn
Design team: B. Edward Balkin, Douglas Dick

Temple Sinai
Design/Completion 1984/1987
Denver, Colorado
Temple Sinai Congregation
Principal in charge of design:
Curtis W. Fentress
Principal in charge of production:
James H. Bradburn
Project designer: B. Edward Balkin
Project manager: John K. McCauley
Design team: Ava Dahlstrom, Dalas Disney, John R. Taylor

Tucson City Center Master Plan
Design 1984
Tucson, Arizona
Reliance Development Group
Principal in charge of design:
Curtis W. Fentress
Principal in charge of production:
James H. Bradburn
Design collaborator: Michael O. Winters

Castlewood Plaza Master Plan
Design 1984
Englewood, Colorado
J. Roulier Interests
Principal in charge of design:
Curtis W. Fentress
Principal in charge of production:
James H. Bradburn
Design team: B. Edward Balkin, Steve Nelson

Mountain Bell Special Services Center
Design 1984
Denver, Colorado
Mountain Bell
Principal in charge of design:
Curtis W. Fentress
Principal in charge of production:
James H. Bradburn
Design team: Deborah R. Allen, Donald W. DeCoster, Annette English, Gregory R. Gidez, Frank G. Hege, JoAnne Hege, James W. O'Neill, Frederick R. Pax, Toshika Yoshida

Pioneer Plaza Hotel
Design 1984
Denver, Colorado
Cambridge Development Group
Principal in charge of design:
Curtis W. Fentress
Principal in charge of production:
James H. Bradburn
Design team: Gary Chamer, Lisa K. Fudge, Gregory R. Gidez, Michael O. Winters

Greenville Park Tower
Design 1984
Dallas, Texas
JRI International/Robert Halloway Corporation
Principal in charge of design:
Curtis W. Fentress
Principal in charge of production:
James H. Bradburn
Project architect: Michael O. Winters
Design team: Garrett M. Christnacht, Steven O. Gregory, Clement Okoye, James W. O'Neill, John R. Taylor

Lexington Center
Design/Completion 1984/1985
Colorado Springs, Colorado
Techkor Development
Principal in charge of design:
Curtis W. Fentress
Principal in charge of production:
James H. Bradburn
Project designer: Brian Chaffee
Project manager: John K. McCauley
Job captain: Patrick M. McKelvey

Norwest Tower
Design/Completion 1984/1986
Tucson, Arizona
Reliance Development Group
Principal in charge of design:
Curtis W. Fentress
Principal in charge of production:
James H. Bradburn
Project designer: Michael O. Winters
Project manager: Stan Kulesa
Design team: Jane Bertschinger, Brian Chaffee, Garrett M. Christnacht, Douglas Dick, Donald W. DeCoster, Gregory R. Gidez, Frank G. Hege, Renata Hajek, John L. Mason, James Niemi, James W. O'Neill, Jim Snyder

Data General Field Engineering Logistics Center
Design/Completion 1984/1986
Fountain, Colorado
Data General Corporation
Principal in charge of design:
Curtis W. Fentress
Principal in charge of production:
James H. Bradburn
Project designer: B. Edward Balkin
Job Captain: John M. Kudrycki
Project manager: Brit Probst
Design team: Garrett M. Christnacht, Frank G. Hege, Renata Hajek, Steven Fritzky

1985

Centennial Office Park Master Plan
Design 1985
Englewood, Colorado
Mission Viejo
Principal in charge of design:
Curtis W. Fentress
Principal in charge of production:
James H. Bradburn
Design team: B. Edward Balkin, Charlotte C. Breed

Parkway Plaza Master Plan
Design 1985
Littleton, Colorado
Talley Corporation
Principal in charge of design:
Curtis W. Fentress
Principal in charge of production:
James H. Bradburn
Design collaborator: Charlotte C. Breed

Fiddler's Green Amphitheater
Design 1985
Englewood, Colorado
John Madden Company
Principal in charge of design:
Curtis W. Fentress
Principal in charge of production:
James H. Bradburn
Design team: Amy Solomon, Galen Bailey, Todd R. Britton

1986

Black American West Museum
Design/Completion 1986/1987
Denver, Colorado
Black America West Museum
Principal in charge of design:
Curtis W. Fentress
Principal in charge of production:
James H. Bradburn
Project architect: James F. Hartman
Design team: Mark Brinkman, Donald W. DeCoster, Mary Jane Koenig, Francis Mishler

Idaho Power Company Corporate Headquarters
Design/Completion 1986/1989
Boise, Idaho
Idaho Power Company
Principal in charge of design:
Curtis W. Fentress
Principal in charge of production:
James H. Bradburn
Architect-of-record: CSHQA Associates
Project architect: Michael O. Winters
Space planning: Sandy Prouty
Design team: Robert G. Datson, Karin Mason, Jack M. Mousseau, Jun Xia

Jefferson County Human Services Building
Design/Completion 1986/1989
Golden, Colorado
Jefferson County, Colorado
Principal in charge of design:
Curtis W. Fentress
Principal in charge of production:
James H. Bradburn
Design team: B. Edward Balkin, Renata Hajek, Barbara K. Hochstetler, John M. Kudrycki, John L. Mason, Mark A. Wagner

Colorado School of Mines
Design/Completion 1986/1990
Golden, Colorado
Colorado School of Mines
Principal in charge of design:
Curtis W. Fentress
Principal in charge of production:
James H. Bradburn
Design team: Robert G. Datson, James F. Hartman, Nancy Kettner, Ned Kirschbaum, Robert Root, Robert Young

Ronstadt Transit Center
Design/Completion 1986/1991
Tucson, Arizona
City of Tucson
Principal in charge of design:
Curtis W. Fentress
Principal in charge of production:
James H. Bradburn
Project designer: Brian Chaffee
Project manager: Robert Louden
Design team: James Carpenter, John L. Mason, Clement Okoye, Robert Root, Michael O. Winters

Jefferson County Government Center Master Plan
Design/Completion 1986/1989-92
Golden, Colorado
Jefferson County, Colorado
Principal in charge of design:
Curtis W. Fentress
Principal in charge of production:
James H. Bradburn
Project architect: B. Edward Balkin
Design collaborator: Brian Chaffee

1987

Sun Plaza
Design 1987
Colorado Springs, Colorado
Sun Resources, Inc.
Principal in charge of design:
Curtis W. Fentress
Principal in charge of production:
James H. Bradburn
Project designer: Luis O. Acosta
Project manager: John K. McCauley
Job captain: Patrick M. McKelvey
Design team: Sandy Brand, Gregory R. Gidez, Frederick R. Pax, John R. Taylor

Boise Civic Center
Design 1987
Boise, Idaho
Dick Holtz
Principal in charge of design:
Curtis W. Fentress
Principal in charge of production:
James H. Bradburn
Project architect: Michael O. Winters

Colorado Convention Center
(Competition)
Design/Completion 1987/1990
Denver, Colorado
City and County of Denver
Principal in charge of design:
Curtis W. Fentress
Principal in charge of production:
James H. Bradburn
Associate architects: Loschky MarQuardt and Nesholm; Bertram A. Bruton and Associates
Project designer: Michael O. Winters
Project manager: Brit Probst
Interior designer: Barbara K. Hochstetler
Design team: B. Edward Balkin, Ronald R. Booth, Richard Burkett, Brian Chaffee, Melanie Colcord, Gregory R. Gidez, Nancy Kettner, John M. Kudrycki, Lauren Lee, Greg Lemon, Beverly G. Pax, John M. Salisbury, Les Stuart, Mark A. Wagner

1988

Oxbridge Town Center
Design 1988
Oxbridge, England
David Sparrow
Principal in charge of design:
Curtis W. Fentress
Principal in charge of production:
James H. Bradburn
Project designer: Michael O. Winters
Design collaborator: Douglas Dick

Denver Permit Center
Design/Completion 1988/1989
Denver, Colorado
City and County of Denver, Colorado
Principal in charge of design:
Curtis W. Fentress
Principal in charge of production:
James H. Bradburn
Design team: James Carpenter, Robert G. Datson, Philip Davis, James F. Hartman, Beverly G. Pax, Frederick R. Pax, Robert Root, John M. Salisbury, Les Stuart

Franklin and Lake
Design/Completion 1988/1989
Chicago, Illinois
Zeller Realty
Principal in charge of design:
Curtis W. Fentress
Principal in charge of production:
James H. Bradburn
Project architect: Michael O. Winters
Design collaborator: Jun Xia

Cherry Creek Plaza
Design/Completion 1988/1990
Denver, Colorado
Bramalea
Principal in charge of design:
Curtis W. Fentress
Principal in charge of production:
James H. Bradburn
Design collaborator: B. Edward Balkin

Jefferson County Government Center Courts and Administration Building
Design/Completion 1988/1993
Golden, Colorado
Jefferson County, Colorado
Principal in charge of design:
Curtis W. Fentress
Principal in charge of production:
James H. Bradburn
Project designer: Brian Chaffee
Project manager: James F. Hartman
Interior designer: Barbara K. Hochstetler
Design team: Gregory D. Billingham, Bill Bramblett, Sandy J. Brand, Richard Burkett, James Carney, James Carpenter, Gregory R. Gidez, Ala F. Hason, Judith Jump, Ned Kirschbaum, Lauren Lee, Robert Louden, John L. Mason, Clement Okoye, Beverly G. Pax, Brit Probst, Samuel Tyner, Mark A. Wagner, Lyn Wisecarver Johnson

1989

Denver Art Museum
(Western and American Galleries)
Design/Completion 1989
Denver, Colorado
Denver Art Museum
Principal in charge of design:
Curtis W. Fentress
Principal in charge of production:
James H. Bradburn
Project managers: Michael Gengler, Robert Root, John M. Salisbury

Estes Park Community and Conference Center
Design/Completion 1989/1991
Estes Park, Colorado
Town of Estes Park, Colorado
Principal in charge of design:
Curtis W. Fentress
Principal in charge of production:
James H. Bradburn
Architect-of-record: Thorpe and Associates
Principal-in-charge: Roger Thorpe
Project architect: Christopher A. Carvell
Project manager: Mark A. Wagner
Interior designer: Barbara K. Hochstetler

University of Colorado Mathematics Building/Gemmill Engineering Sciences Library
Design/Completion 1989/1992
Boulder, Colorado
University of Colorado
Principal in charge of design:
Curtis W. Fentress
Principal in charge of production:
James H. Bradburn
Project designer: Christopher A. Carvell
Project architect: Robert Louden
Interior designer: Gary Morris
Project manager: Nancy Kettner
Design team: Douglas Eichelberger, Greg Lemon, Michael O. Winters, Jun Xia

Natural Resources Laboratory and Administration Building (Competition)
Design/Completion 1989/1992
Olympia, Washington
State of Washington, General Services Administration
Principal in charge of design:
Curtis W. Fentress
Principal in charge of production:
James H. Bradburn
Project architect: Ronald R. Booth
Interior designer: Barbara K. Hochstetler
Project manager: John M. Kudrycki
Job captain: Gregory R. Gidez
Design team: James Carney, Milan Hart, Arthur A. Hoy, III, Lyn Wisecarver Johnson, Lauren Lee, David Tompkins, Michael Wisneski

Colorado State Capitol Life-Safety Project
Design/Completion 1989/1999
Denver, Colorado
State of Colorado
Principal in charge of design:
Curtis W. Fentress
Principal in charge of production:
James H. Bradburn
Project architect: James F. Hartman
Design team: Garrett M Christnacht, Ala F. Hason, Brian Ostler, John M. Salisbury, Samuel Tyner

1990

Westlake Residences
Design 1990
Seattle, Washington
Astral Investments
Principal in charge of design:
Curtis W. Fentress
Principal in charge of production:
James H. Bradburn
Project architect: Christopher A. Carvell
Project manager: Mark A. Wagner
Design team: Richard Burkett, Peter D. Carlson

809 Olive Way
Design 1990
Seattle, Washington
Western Securities Ltd.
Principal in charge of design:
Curtis W. Fentress
Principal in charge of production:
James H. Bradburn
Project architect: Christopher A. Carvell
Project manager: Mark A. Wagner
Design team: Ronald R. Booth, Robert Louden

Denver Central Library and Urban Analysis
Design 1990
Denver, Colorado
City and County of Denver, Colorado
Principal in charge of design:
Curtis W. Fentress
Principal in charge of production:
James H. Bradburn
Design team: Arthur A. Hoy, III, Michel Pariseau

Union Station Redevelopment Plan
Design 1990–91
Denver, Colorado
Union Station Redevelopment Committee
Principal in charge of design:
Curtis W. Fentress
Principal in charge of production:
James H. Bradburn
Design team: Galen Bailey, Todd R. Britton, Arthur A. Hoy, III

IBM Customer Service Center
Design/Completion 1990/1992
Boulder, Colorado
IBM
Principal in charge of design:
Curtis W. Fentress
Principal in charge of production:
James H. Bradburn
Project designer: Barbara K. Hochstetler
Project manager: Donald W. DeCoster
Design team: Robert G. Datson, Kathleen Corner Galvin, John A. Gossett, Judith Jump, Sandy Prouty, Michael O. Winters

1991

Cathedral Square
Design 1991
Milwaukee, Wisconsin
Corum Real Estate Group
Principal in charge of design:
Curtis W. Fentress
Principal in charge of production:
James H. Bradburn
Design team: Peter D. Carlson

University Art Museum
(University of California at Santa Barbara)
Design 1991
Santa Barbara, California
University of California at Santa Barbara
Principal in charge of design:
Curtis W. Fentress
Principal in charge of production:
James H. Bradburn
Associate architect: John Prosser
Project architect: Michael O. Winters
Design collaborator: Douglas Dick

Denver International Airport Passenger Terminal Complex
Design/Completion 1991/1994
Denver, Colorado
City and County of Denver
Principal in charge of design:
Curtis W. Fentress
Principal in charge of production:
James H. Bradburn
Associate architect: Pouw and Associates Inc.; Bertram A. Bruton and Associates
Project architect: Michael O. Winters
Project manager: Thomas J. Walsh
Interior designer: Barbara K. Hochstetler
Project director: Brit Probst
Job captains: Joseph Solomon, John M. Salisbury
Design team: Galen Bailey, Todd R. Britton, Richard Burkett, James Carney, James Carpenter, Brian Chaffee, Garrett M. Christnacht, John Gagnon, Kathleen Galvin, Michael Gengler, Gregory R. Gidez, Warren Hogue, III, Doris Hung, Charles Johns, Anthia Kappos, Michael Klebba, John M. Kudrycki, Lauren Lee, Robert Louden, Michael Miller, Gary Morris, Jack M. Mousseau, A. Chris Olson, Brian Ostler, Teri Paris, Frederick R. Pax, Robert Root, Tim Roush, Amy Solomon, Les Stuart, Dave Tompkins, Samuel Tyner, Mark A. Wagner, John C. Wurzenberger, Jr., Jun Xia

National Museum of Wildlife Art
(Competition)
Design/Completion 1991/1995
Jackson Hole, Wyoming
National Museum of Wildlife Art/Bill and Joffa Kerr
Principal in charge of design:
Curtis W. Fentress
Principal in charge of production:
James H. Bradburn
Project architect: Brian Chaffee
Interior designer: Gary Morris
Job captain: Gregory R. Gidez
Design team: Anthia Kappos, Brian Ostler, Tim Roush

National Cowboy Hall of Fame Renovation/Expansion (Competition)
Design/Completion 1991/1997
Oklahoma City, Oklahoma
National Cowboy Hall of Fame
Principal in charge of design:
Curtis W. Fentress
Principal in charge of production:
James H. Bradburn
Project architect: Ronald R. Booth
Interior designer: Barbara K. Hochstetler
Project manager: Mark A. Wagner
Job captain: Gregory D. Billingham
Design team: Peter D. Carlson, John Gagnon, John M. McGahey, Gary Morris, Jack M. Mousseau, Teri Paris, Thomas P. Theobald

1992

Dinosaur Discovery Museum
Design 1992
Canyon City, Colorado
Garden Park Paleontological Society
Principal in charge of design:
Curtis W. Fentress
Principal in charge of production:
James H. Bradburn
Project architect: Brian Chaffee
Design team: Carl J. Dalio, Wilbur Moore

West Hills Hotel
Design 1992
Keystone, Colorado
Chamer Development
Principal in charge of design:
Curtis W. Fentress
Principal in charge of production:
James H. Bradburn
Project architect: Michael O. Winters
Project manager: Brit Probst
Design team: Gary Chamer, Mark A. Wagner

Eastbank Conference Center and Hotel
Design 1992
Wichita, Kansas
Ross Investment
Principal in charge of design:
Curtis W. Fentress
Principal in charge of production:
James H. Bradburn
Project architect: Mark A. Wagner
Interior designer: Barbara K. Hochstetler

Colorado Convention Center Hotel
Design 1992
Denver, Colorado
J. Roulier Interests
Principal in charge of design:
Curtis W. Fentress
Principal in charge of production:
James H. Bradburn
Design team: Galen Bailey, Todd R. Britton, Amy Solomon, Jun Xia

Coors Field
Design 1992
Denver, Colorado
Denver Metropolitan Major League Baseball Stadium District Commission
Principal in charge of design:
Curtis W. Fentress
Principal in charge of production:
James H. Bradburn
Associate architect: Ellerbe Becket, Inc.
Design team: John A. Gossett, Michael Pariseau

Kuala Lumpur Airport
Design 1992
Kuala Lumpu
McClier Aviation Group
Principal in charge of design:
Curtis W. Fentress
Principal in charge of production:
James H. Bradburn
Design team: Carl J. Dalio, Michael O. Winters

Moscow Redevelopment Project
Design 1992
Moscow, Russia
Moscow Redevelopment Group
Principal in charge of design:
Curtis W. Fentress
Principal in charge of production:
James H. Bradburn
Associate architect: Andrei Meerson & Partners
Design team: Arthur A. Hoy, III, Jack M. Mousseau, Aleksandr Sheykhet, Michael O. Winters

Catalina Resort Community
Design 1992
Playa Dantita, Ocotal, Costa Rica
Developments International, Inc.
Principal in charge of design:
Curtis W. Fentress
Principal in charge of production:
James H. Bradburn
Project designer: Jack M. Mousseau
Project manager: Barbara K. Hochstetler
Design collaborator: Wilbur Moore

Clark County Master Plan
Design 1992
Las Vegas, Nevada
Clark County General Services Department
Principal in charge of design:
Curtis W. Fentress
Principal in charge of production:
James H. Bradburn
Design team: Arthur A. Hoy, III,
Michael O. Winters

Clark County Government Center
(Competition)
Design/Completion 1992/1995
Las Vegas, Nevada
Clark County General Services Department
Principal in charge of design:
Curtis W. Fentress
Principal in charge of production:
James H. Bradburn
Associate architect: Domingo Cambeiro Corporation
Project architect: Michael O. Winters
Interior designer: Barbara K. Hochstetler
Project manager: John M. Kudrycki
Job captain: Ned Kirschbaum
Design team: Ronald R. Booth, John A. Gossett, Ala F. Hason, Warren Hogue, III, Arthur A. Hoy, III, Anthia Kappos, Lauren Lee, Robert Louden, Gary Morris, Joy Spatz, Michael Wisneski, John C. Wurzenberger, Jr.

David E. Skaggs Federal Building
(National Oceanic and Atmospheric Administration Boulder Research Laboratories)
Design/Completion 1992/1998
Boulder, Colorado
United States General Services Administration/National Oceanic and Atmospheric Administration
Principal in charge of design:
Curtis W. Fentress
Principal in charge of production:
James H. Bradburn
Project architect: Ronald R. Booth
Interior designer: Barbara K. Hochstetler
Project manager: Jeffrey W. Olson
Design team: Peter D. Carlson, Gregory R. Gidez, Ala F. Hason, Warren Hogue, III, Robert Louden, Gary Morris, Teri Paris

1993

Vladivostok City Center
Design 1993
Vladivostok, Russia
Jupiter Development
Principal in charge of design:
Curtis W. Fentress
Principal in charge of production:
James H. Bradburn
Project architect: Arthur A. Hoy, III
Design team: Doni Mitchell, Aleksandr Sheykhet

Second Bangkok International Airport
(Competition)
Design 1993
Bangkok, Thailand
Airport Authority of Thailand
Principal in charge of design:
Curtis W. Fentress
Principal in charge of production:
James H. Bradburn
Associate architect: McClier Aviation Group
Project designer: Michael O. Winters
Interior designer: Barbara K. Hochstetler
Project architect: Jack M. Mousseau
Project manager: Thomas J. Walsh
Design team: Galen Bailey, Nina Bazian, Todd R. Britton, Catherine Dunn, David Goorman, John A. Gossett, John M. McGahey, Doni Mitchell, Gary Morris, Minh Nguyen, Brian Ostler, Amy Solomon, Voraporn Sundarupura

Kwangju Bank Headquarters
Design 1993
Kwangju, Republic of South Korea
Kwangju Bank
Principal in charge of design:
Curtis W. Fentress
Principal in charge of production:
James H. Bradburn
Design collaborator: Arthur A. Hoy, III

David Eccles Conference Center and Peery's Egyptian Theater
Design/Completion 1993/1996
Ogden, Utah
Weber County, Utah
Principal in charge of design:
Curtis W. Fentress
Principal in charge of production:
James H. Bradburn
Architect-of-record: Sanders Herman Associates
Project designer: Ronald R. Booth
Project architect: Christopher A. Carvell
Project managers: Mark A. Wagner
Design team: Gregory D. Billingham, Peter D. Carlson, Robert Herman, Michael Sanders, Thomas P. Theobald

Colorado Christian Home/Tennyson Center for Children and Families
Design/Completion 1993/1996
Denver, Colorado
National Benevolent Association
Principal in charge of design:
Curtis W. Fentress
Principal in charge of production:
James H. Bradburn
Project architect: Arthur A. Hoy, III
Technical coordinator: Gregory R. Gidez
Design team: John Gagnon, Warren Hogue, III, Teri Paris

Montrose Government Center
Design/Completion 1993/1997
Montrose, Colorado
Montrose County, Colorado
Principal in charge of design:
Curtis W. Fentress
Principal in charge of production:
James H. Bradburn
Associate architect: Reilly Johnson, Architects
Project architect: Christopher A. Carvell
Project designer: Brian Chaffee
Design team: Doni Mitchell, Aleksandr Sheykhet

Gunter Hall Renovation
(University of Northern Colorado)
Design/Completion 1993/1997
Greeley, Colorado
University of Northern Colorado
Principal in charge of design:
Curtis W. Fentress
Principal in charge of production:
James H. Bradburn
Design team: Christopher A. Carvell, John Conklin, James F. Hartman, Lauren Lee

1994

The Reconstruction of the Souks of Beirut: An International Ideas Competition
Design 1994
Beirut, Lebanon
Solidere
Principal in charge of design:
Curtis W. Fentress
Principal in charge of production:
James H. Bradburn
Associate architect: Saudi Diyar Consultants
Project manager: Michael Wisneski
Project architect: Ala F. Hason
Architectural historian: Roger A. Chandler
Researcher: Mark T. Harpe
Design team: Nina Bazian, Jamili Butros Copty, Yasser R. Kaaki, Jack M. Mousseau, Minh Nguyen, Voraporn Sundarupura

Hawaii Convention Center
Design 1994
Honolulu, Hawaii
State of Hawaii
Principal in charge of design:
Curtis W. Fentress
Principal in charge of production:
James H. Bradburn
Associate architects: DMJM Hawaii; Kauahikaua and Chun Associates
Project architect: Michael O. Winters
Project manager: John M. Kudrycki
Project designer: Jack M. Mousseau
Interior designer: Gary Morris
Design team: Nina Bazian, Cydney Fisher, Michael Gengler, Haia Ghalib, John A. Gossett, Ala F. Hason, John M. McGahey, Aleksandr Sheykhet, Voraporn Sundarupura, Thomas J. Walsh, John C. Wurzenburger, Jr.

One Polo Creek
Design/Completion 1994/1997
Cherry Creek, Colorado
BCORP Holdings and AIMCO
Principal in charge of design:
Curtis W. Fentress
Principal in charge of production:
James H. Bradburn
Project designer: Christopher A. Carvell
Project architects: Robert Louden, John C. Wurzenburger, Jr.
Design team: Gregory D. Billingham, Richard Burkett, William B. Buyers, Peter D. Carlson, Garrett M. Christnacht, Jayne Coburn, Marc Dietrick, Catherine Dunn, Jane Hiley, Warren Hogue, III, Arthur A. Hoy, III, Charles Johns, Patrick Keefe, Jamie LaCasse, Gregory Lockridge, Robert Louden, Jack M. Mousseau, Scott Martin, Michael Miller, Gary Morris, A. Chris Olson, Mark Rothman, Aleksandr Sheykhet, James Sobey, Michael Stesney, Les Stuart, Alexa Taylor, Thomas P. Theobald, Alexander Thome', Paul Tylar, Mark A. Wagner, Marilyn White, Michael Wisneski, John C. Wurzenburger, Jr.

Seoul Inchon International Airport Passenger Terminal Complex
(Competition)
Design/Completion 1994/2000
Seoul, Republic of South Korea
Korean Airports Authority
Principal in charge of design:
Curtis W. Fentress
Principal in charge of production:
James H. Bradburn
Associate architect: Korean Architects Collaborative International (KACI)
Project architect: Jack M. Mousseau
Interior designer: Barbara K. Hochstetler
Project director: Thomas J. Walsh
Job captain: Richard Burkett
Design team: Galen Bailey, Todd R. Britton, Richard Burkett, Jack Cook, John Gagnon, Arthur A. Hoy, III, Anthia Kappos, Ned Kirschbaum, Lauren Lee, Scott Martin, John M. McGahey, Wilbur Moore, Gary Morris, Brian Ostler, Mark Outman, Michelle Ray, Tim Roush, Amy Solomon, Les Stuart, Michael O. Winters, John C. Wurzenberger, Jr.

1995

3883 Howard Hughes Parkway
(Competition)
Design/Completion 1995/2000
Las Vegas, Nevada
The Howard Hughes Corporation
Principal in charge of design:
Curtis W. Fentress
Principal in charge of production:
James H. Bradburn
Design team: Michael O. Winters, Jack Mousseau, Peter Carlson

One Wynkoop Plaza
Design/Completion 1995/1997
Denver, Colorado
Thermo Development L.L.C.
Principal in charge of design:
Curtis W. Fentress
Principal in charge of production:
James H. Bradburn
Associate architect: Shears-Leese Associated Architects
Project designer: Brian Chaffee
Design team: Catherine Dunn, Charles Johns, Jack Mousseau, Alexander Sheyket

The Dunbar Resort
Design/Completion 1995/1998
Deadwood, South Dakota
The Dunbar Resort
Principal in charge of design:
Curtis W. Fentress
Principal in charge of production:
James H. Bradburn
Design architect: Hill/Glazier Architects, Inc.
Project designer: Robert Glazier
Project manager: John M. Kudrycki
Design team: Warren Hogue, III, Ned Kirschbaum, Robert Louden, Scott Martin, A. Chris Olson, Robert Riffel, Alexa Taylor, Thomas P. Theobald, Alexander Thome'

City of Oakland Administration Buildings
(Competition)
Design/Completion 1995/1998
Oakland, California
City of Oakland
Principal in charge of design:
Curtis W. Fentress
Principal in charge of production:
James H. Bradburn
Associate architects: Muller & Caulfield, Gerson/Overstreet, Y.H. Lee
Project architect: Ronald R. Booth
Project designers: Ronald R. Booth, Peter D. Carlson, Catherine Dunn, Mark Outman
Project manager: Jeff Olson
Design team: John Conklin, Gregory R. Gidez, Warren Hogue, III, Kristen Hurty, Gregory Lockridge, Michael Miller, Jack M. Mousseau, Trey Warren, Michael O. Winters, Jacqueline Wisniewski, Monica Barrasa, Shannon Cody, Barbara Fentress

Cathedral City Civic Center
(Competition)
Design 1995
Cathedral City, California
City of Cathedral City
Associate architect: Donald A. Wexler
Principal in charge of design:
Curtis W. Fentress
Principal in charge of production:
James H. Bradburn
Design team: Jim Sobey, Cydney McGlothlin

The Bank Lofts
Design 1995
Denver, Colorado
National Properties
Principal in charge of design:
Curtis W. Fentress
Principal in charge of production:
James H. Bradburn
Project architect: Joseph Solomon
Project manager: Jim Hartman
Job captain: John C. Wurzenberger, Jr.
Design collaborator: Brian Ostler

1996

The Design AEC Competition 1996
(Bentley Systems, Inc.)
Design 1996
Long Beach, California
The Ratkovich Company
Principal in charge of design:
Curtis W. Fentress
Principal in charge of production:
James H. Bradburn
Project designer: Deborah Lucking
Project manager: Mark Rothman
Design team: Ned Kirschbaum, Petr Dostal, Cydney Fisher, Haia Ghalib, Scott Martin, Mark McGlothlin

DIA Westin Hotel
Design 1996
Denver, Colorado
DIA Development Corporation
Principal in charge of design:
Curtis W. Fentress
Principal in charge of production:
James H. Bradburn
Design team: Brian Chaffee, James Sobey, Thomas J. Walsh, Kristen Hurty, Cydney Fisher

The Tritch Building and the Rialto Café
Design/Completion 1996/1998
Denver, Colorado
Sage Hospitality Resources
Principal in charge of design:
Curtis W. Fentress
Principal in charge of production:
James H. Bradburn
Design team: Jim Hartman, Warren Hogue, Petr Dostal, Bret Johnson, Joseph Solomon, John Kudrycki, Ronald R. Booth, Marc Dietrick, Jim Johnson, Mark Wagner, Greg Gidez, Irina Mokrova, Kristen Hurty, Robin D. Ault

ICG Communications Corporate Headquarters
Design/Completion 1996/1997
Englewood, Colorado
ICG Communications, Inc.
Design architect: W. Stephen Wood
Principal in charge of design:
Curtis W. Fentress
Principal in charge of production:
James H. Bradburn
Project architect: Michael O. Winters
Project manager: John M. Kudrycki
Design team: William B. Buyers, Todd R. Britton, Robert Riffel, Alekandr Sheykhet, Amy Soloman, Alexander Thome', Jacqueline Wisniewski

J.D. Edwards & Co. Corporate Headquarters
Design/Completion 1996/1997
Denver, Colorado
J.D. Edwards and Company
Principal in charge of design:
Curtis W. Fentress
Principal in charge of production:
James H. Bradburn
Project designer: Ronald R. Booth
Project manager: Jeff Olson
Job captain: Robert Louden
Design team: Robin D. Ault, Garrett M. Christnacht, Haia Ghalib, David Harmon, Warren Hogue, III, Sanjeev Molhatra, Robert Riffel, Alexander Thome'
Interiors project manager: John C. Wurzenberger, Jr.
Interiors project designer: Jamie LaCasse

Gulf Canada Resources Ltd (Interiors)
Design/Completion 1996/1997
Denver, Colorado
Gulf Canada Resources, Limited
Principals-in-charge of Design:
Curtis W. Fentress and Michael O. Winters
Principal in charge of production:
James H. Bradburn
Project designer: Jamie LaCasse
Project manager: John C. Wurzenburger, Jr.
Design team: Shannon Cody, Cydney Fisher, Ali Gidfar, David Harman, Brent Mather, Mark McGlothlin, Irina Mokrova

Regional Transportation Commission and Regional Flood Control District Headquarters and Administrative Center
Design/Completion 1996/1998
Las Vegas, Nevada
Regional Transportation Commission
Associate architect: Robert A. Fielden
Principal in charge of design:
Curtis W. Fentress
Principal in charge of production:
James H. Bradburn
Design principal: Michael O. Winters
Design team: Robert Riffel, Robert Louden, Brent Mather, Sanjeev Malhotra, Todd R. Britton, Amy Solomon

Palmetto Bay Beach Resort
Design/Completion 1996/1999
Roatan, Honduras
Roatan Development Group
Principal in charge of design:
Curtis W. Fentress
Principal in charge of production:
James H. Bradburn
Project designer: James Sobey
Project collaborator: Brian Chaffee

The New Doha International Airport
(Competition)
Design/Completion 1996/2000
Doha, Qatar
Ministry of Municipal Affairs and Agriculture
Principal in charge of design:
Curtis W. Fentress
Principal in charge of production:
James H. Bradburn
Project designer: Jack M. Mousseau
Project manager: Ned Kirschbaum
Design team: Thomas J. Walsh, Jack Cook, Mark Outman, Thomas P. Theobald, Deborah Lucking, Alexander Thomé, Haia Ghalib, Robert Riffel, Valerie Slack, Alexa Taylor, Mike Miller, Garrett M. Christnacht, Shannon Cody, Tina DuMond, Gregory Lockridge, Scott Martin, Jacqueline Wisniewski, Bradly Wonnacott

1997

**La Nueva Área Terminal del Aeropuerto Madrid/Barajas
(New Terminal Area for Madrid/Barajas International Airport)**
(Competition)
Design 1997
Madrid, Spain
Aeropuertos Espanoles y Navegacion Aerea (AENA)
Principal in charge of design:
Curtis W. Fentress
Design team: Ronald R. Booth, Thomas J. Walsh, Kristoffer Kenton, Robin D. Ault, Mark McGlothlin, Cydney McGlothlin, Mark Outman, Todd Britton, Amy Solomon, John Rollo, Brent Mather, Haia Ghalib

Complex Suria Merdeka
(Kuching Town Centre)
Design/Completion 1997/2004
Kuching, Sarawak, Malaysia
HAL Development Son. Bhd. (Kuala Lumpur)
Principal in charge of design:
Curtis W. Fentress
Principal in charge of production:
James H. Bradburn
Project designer: Mark Outman
Design collaborator: Haia Ghalib

Terminal 2, Flughafen München (Second Terminal Munich Airport) (Competition)
Design/Completion 1997/1998
Munich, Germany
Flughafen München
Principal in charge of design:
Curtis W. Fentress
Principal in charge of production:
James H. Bradburn
Project designer: Jack Mousseau
Design team: Will Moore, Robin D. Ault, Cydney McGlothlin, Mark McGlothlin

3993 Howard Hughes Parkway
(Competition)
Design/Completion 1997/1999
Las Vegas, Nevada
The Howard Hughes Corporation
Principal in charge of design:
Curtis W. Fentress
Principal in charge of production:
James H. Bradburn
Design principal: Michael O. Winters
Design team: Jack Cook, Robert Riffel, Sanjeev Malhotra, Robert Louden, Brent Mather, Mark Outman

Midway Office Complex and Master Plan
Design 1997
Memphis, Tennessee
Private Corporation
Principal in charge of design:
Curtis W. Fentress
Principal in charge of production:
James H. Bradburn
Design team: Ronald R. Booth, Cydney McGlothlin, Mark McGlothlin

Kuala Lumpur Hotel and Office Complex
Design/Completion 1997/2000
Kuala Lumpur, Malaysia
Hiap Aik Construction Berhad
Principal in charge of design:
Curtis W. Fentress
Principal in charge of production:
James H. Bradburn
Project designer: James Sobey
Project manager: Greg D. Billingham

Presidio Town Center
Design/Completion 1997/2000
San Francisco, California
Bayshore Properties, Inc.
Principal in charge of design:
Curtis W. Fentress
Principal in charge of production:
James H. Bradburn
Project designer: James Sobey

Goldrush Casino
Design/Completion 1997/2000
Central City, Colorado
Dynasty Corporation Hotel and Casino
Principal in charge of design:
Curtis W. Fentress
Principal in charge of production:
James H. Bradburn
Project manager: Jack Cook
Design team: Arthur A. Hoy, III, Jack M. Mousseau

Deira Bus Station and Car Park (Competition)
Design/Completion 1997/2000
Dubai, United Arab Emirates
Dubai Municipality
Principal in charge of design:
Curtis W. Fentress
Principal in charge of production:
James H. Bradburn
Associate architect: Dar Al-Handasah Shair and Partners
Project designer: Brian Chaffee
Design team: William B. Buyers, Deborah Lucking

Blackhawk Casino
Design 1997
Black Hawk, Colorado
Riviera Hotel
Principal in charge of design:
Curtis W. Fentress
Principal in charge of production:
James H. Bradburn
Project manager: Jack Cook
Project designer: Jack Mousseau

Citibank/Citicorp Diners Club (Interiors)
Design/Completion 1997/1999
Englewood, Colorado
Citicorp Realty Services
Principal in charge of design:
Curtis W. Fentress
Principal in charge of production:
James H. Bradburn
Project manager: Greg Gidez
Design team: Joseph Solomon, Irina Mokrova

1998

The Birdhouse Project 1998
Design 1998
Osaka, Japan
The Birdhouse Project Executive Committee
Principal in charge of design:
Curtis W. Fentress
Design team: Deborah Lucking, Delia Esquivel, Todd Britton, Amy Solomon, John Rollo

3790 Howard Hughes Parkway
Design/Completion 1998/TBD
Las Vegas, Nevada
The Howard Hughes Corporation
Principal in charge of design:
Curtis W. Fentress
Principal in charge of production:
James H. Bradburn
Design team: Michael O. Winters, Mark Outman, Robin D. Ault

Larimer County Justice Center (Competition)
Design/Completion 1998/2000
Fort Collins, Colorado
Larimer County Commissioners
Principal in charge of design:
Curtis W. Fentress
Principal in charge of production:
James H. Bradburn
Project architect: Brian Chaffee
Project manager: Greg Billingham
Project team: Mike Stesney, Charles Johns, Kristen Hurty, Jacqueline Wisniewski, Delia Esquivel, Chris Boal, Kristoffer Kenton

Buffalo Bill Historical Center
Design/Completion 1998/2000
Cody, Wyoming
Buffalo Bill Historical Center
Principal in charge of design:
Curtis W. Fentress
Principal in charge of production:
James H. Bradburn
Project architect: Mike Miller
Project designer: Ronald R. Booth
Project manager: Mark Wagner
Interior design: Jamie LaCasse
Design team: Deborah Lucking, Robin D. Ault, Kristen Hurty, Cydney McGlothlin, Robert Riffel, Robert Savi, Loree Karr, Megan Walsh, Weskeal West, Jacqueline Wisniewski, Christina Cortright, Sonny Willier

Madrid/Barajas Technical Services
Design/Completion 1998/1999
Madrid, Spain
Aeropuertos Espanoles y Navegacion Aerea (AENA)
Principal in charge of design:
Curtis W. Fentress
Project architect and airport planner:
Thomas J. Walsh
Design team: Joseph Solomon, Cydney McGlothlin, Heinrich E. Wirth

Denver Academy
Design/Completion 1998/2001
Denver, Colorado
Denver Academy
Principal in charge of design:
Curtis W. Fentress
Principal in charge of production:
James H. Bradburn
Project manager: Thomas P. Theobald
Design team: Derek Starkenburg, Valerie Slack, Irina Mokrova, Jim Johnson, Mark Outman

Seattle-Tacoma International Airport Central Terminal Expansion
Design/Completion 1998/2004
Seattle, Washington
Port of Seattle
Principal in charge of design:
Curtis W. Fentress
Principal in charge of production:
James H. Bradburn
Project manager: Thomas J. Walsh
Project designer: Jack Mousseau
Project architect: Ned Kirschbaum
Design team: Mike Miller, Marc Dietrick, Mark Outman, Kristen Hurty, Robert Riffel, Deborah Lucking, Christina Cortright, Pete Akins, Jason Loui, Robin D. Ault, Derek Starkenburg, Todd Britton, Amy Solomon, John Rollo

Civic Center Parking Structure
(Competition)
Design/Completion 1998/1999
Fort Collins, Colorado
City of Fort Collins
Principal in charge of design:
Curtis W. Fentress
Principal in charge of production:
James H. Bradburn
Project architect: Brian Chaffee
Project team: Alexa Taylor, Brent Mather

Bronco Stadium
Design/Completion 1998/2001
Denver, Colorado
Denver Broncos
Architect: HNTB Sports Entertainment
Associate architects: Fentress Bradburn, Bertram A. Bruton Associates
Principal in charge of design:
Curtis W. Fentress
Principal in charge of production:
James H. Bradburn
Project architect: Mark Outman
Project manager: Greg Gidez
Design team: Alexa Taylor, Charles Johns, Tim Geisler, Nejeeb Khan, Rick Talley, Jack Mousseau, Felipe Pineiro, Nathan James, Kelsi Billingham, Scott Allen, Delia Esquivel, John Kudrycki, Mark McGlothlin, Tom Theobald, Alex Thomé, Robin D. Ault

Lucent Technologies (Interiors)
Design/Completion 1998/2001
Highlands Ranch, Colorado
Lucent Technologies
Principal in charge of design:
Curtis W. Fentress
Principal in charge of production:
James H. Bradburn
Project manager: John C. Wurzenberger, Jr.
Design team: Michael O. Winters, Lauren Lee, Jonathan Coppin, Jack Cook, Rex Canady, Christina Cortright, Delia Esquivel

Smith, Brooks, Bolshoun & Co.
Design/Completion 1998/1999
Denver, Colorado
Smith, Brooks, Bolshoun & Co.
Principal in charge of design:
Curtis W. Fentress
Principal in charge of production:
James H. Bradburn
Project manager: Mark Wagner
Project architect: Joseph Solomon
Project collaborator: John C. Wurzenberger, Jr.

1999

Research Complex I (University of Colorado Health Sciences Center)
Design/Completion 1999/2004
Denver, Colorado
University Colorado Health Sciences Center
Associate architect: Kling Lindquist
Principal in charge of design:
Curtis W. Fentress
Principal in charge of production:
James H. Bradburn
Project architect: Jack Cook
Project manager: Jeff Olson
Design team: Scott Allen, Ronald R. Booth, Rex Canady, Garret Christnacht, Antonio

Kuwait Finance House Tower
Design/Completion 1999/2002
Kuwait City, Kuwait
The Kuwaiti Manager Company
Principal in charge of design:
Curtis W. Fentress
Project architect: Ned Kirschbaum
Project designer: Kristoffer Kenton
Design collaborator: Mark Outman

Flughafen Wien (Vienna Airport)
(Competition)
Design 1999
Vienna, Austria
City of Vienna
Principal in charge of design:
Curtis W. Fentress
Project designer: Kristoffer Kenton
Airport planner: Thomas J. Walsh
Design team: Will Moore, Brigitte Routhfuss

ICE Terminal Köln-Deutz/Messe (Cologne Convention Center Train Station)
(Competition)
Design 1999
Cologne, Germany
Deutsche Bahn
Principal in charge of design:
Curtis W. Fentress
Principal in charge of production:
James H. Bradburn
Design team: Kristoffer Kenton, Will Moore

Fiddler's Green Center Building II
Design/Completion 1999/2001
Englewood, Colorado
The John Madden Company
Principal in charge of design:
Curtis W. Fentress
Principal in charge of production:
James H. Bradburn
Associate principal: Jack Mousseau
Senior associate: Ned Kirschbaum
Project architect: Catherine Dunn

Cherry Creek South Condominiums
Design/Completion 1999/2001
Denver, Colorado
Raymond Williams Construction
Principal in charge of design:
Curtis W. Fentress
Principal in charge of production:
James H. Bradburn
Project architect: Brian Chaffee
Design collaborator: Chris Boal

421 Broadway
Design/Completion 1999/2001
Denver, Colorado
Fentress Bradburn Architects Ltd.
Principal in charge of design:
Curtis W. Fentress
Principal in charge of production:
James H. Bradburn
Design team: Jim Sobey, Joseph Solomon, Jim Johnson, Natalie Lucero

M-E Engineers Building
Design/Completion 1999/2000
Wheat Ridge, Colorado
M-E Engineers, Inc.
Principal in charge of design:
Curtis W. Fentress
Principal in charge of production:
James H. Bradburn
Project architect: Robert Louden
Design team: Jonathan Coppin, Jamie LaCasse, Nejeeb Khan

Central California History Museum
(Competition)
Design 1999
Fresno, California
Fresno City and County Historical Society
Principal in charge of design:
Curtis W. Fentress
Principal in charge of production:
James H. Bradburn
Project architect: Brian Chaffee
Design team: Derek Starkenburg, Nejeebkhan Rayammarakkar

Colorado Christian University
(Competition)
Design 1998
Lakewood, Colorado
Colorado Christian University
Principal in charge of design:
Curtis W. Fentress
Project architect: Brian Chaffee
Design team: Kristoffer Kenton, John Rollo, Robin D. Ault, Derek Starkenburg

2000

Colorado Convention Center Expansion
Design/Completion 2000/2004
Denver, Colorado
City of Denver
Associate Architects: Bertram A. Bruton Associates, Harold Massop Associates
Principal in charge of design:
Curtis W. Fentress
Principal in charge of production:
James H. Bradburn
Design team: Michael O. Winters, Robin D. Ault, Robert Riffel, Mark Outman, John Kudrycki, Todd R. Britton, Amy Solomon, John Rollo

Air Zoo at Kalamazoo
Design/Completion 2000/TBD
Kalamazoo, Michigan
Kalamazoo Aviation History Museum
Associate architect: Wigen Tincknell Meyer & Associates
Exhibit design: DMCD
Principal in charge of design:
Curtis W. Fentress
Principal in charge of production:
James H. Bradburn
Project designer: Ronald R. Booth
Project manager: Mark Wagner
Design team: Alex Thomé, Kristen Hurty, Sonny Willier, Melissa Parker, Jacqueline Wisniewski, Christina Cortright

Janus Corporate Campus
Design/Completion 2000/2003
Denver, Colorado
Janus Facilities
Principal in charge of design:
Curtis W. Fentress
Principal in charge of production:
James H. Bradburn
Project architect: Mark Outman
Design team: Robert Louden, Jacqueline Wisniewski, Natalie Lucero

Loveland Police and Courts Building
Design/Completion 2000/2001
Loveland, Colorado
City of Loveland
Principal in charge of design:
Curtis W. Fentress
Principal in charge of production:
James H. Bradburn
Project principal: Brian Chaffee
Project manager: Greg Billingham
Design team: Rick Talley, Charles Johns, Garret Christnacht, Rex Canady, Delia Esquivel, Nejeeb Khan, Jacqueline Wisniewski

Capitol Area - East End Campus
Design/Completion 2000/2002
Sacramento, California
State of California
Principal in charge of production:
James H. Bradburn
Project architect: Robert Louden
Project manager: Greg Gidez
Project designer: Deborah Tan Lucking
Design team: Carl Goodiel, Deborah Goodiel, Felipe Pineiro, Rick Talley, Brad Wonnacott, Chris Boal, Rex Canady

Colorado State Capitol Life-Safety Renovation
Design/Completion 2000/2005
Denver, Colorado
State of Colorado
Principal in charge of design:
Curtis W. Fentress
Principal in charge of production:
James H. Bradburn
Project manager: John C. Wurzenberger, Jr.
Design team: Brian Chaffee, Jim Johnson, Rafael Espinoza, Jason Loui, Joseph Solomon

Cherry Hills Community Church Chapel
Design/Completion 2000/2002
Highlands Ranch, Colorado
Cherry Hills Community Church
Principal in charge of design:
Curtis W. Fentress
Principal in charge of production:
James H. Bradburn
Design team: James A. Sobey, Derek Starkenburg

Sacramento High Rise Lot A
Design 2000
Sacramento, California
David Taylor
Principal in charge of design:
Curtis W. Fentress
Project designer: Mark Outman

Colorado History Museum Expansion
Design 1998, 2000
Denver, Colorado
Colorado Historical Society
Principal in charge of design:
Curtis W. Fentress
Principal in charge of production:
James H. Bradburn
Design team: Haia Ghalib, Kristoffer Kenton, John Rollo

Selected Bibliography

2000
Dubbs, Dana. "Oakland Reinvents Itself," *Facilities Design & Management*, January 2000.

Weiser, Nora. "The Nation's Biggest Landlord Just Found Style," *Architectural Record*, February 2000.

Sommers, Jessica. *Gateway to the West: Designing the Passenger Terminal Complex at Denver International Airport*, The Images Publishing Group, 2000.

1999
Vitta, Maurizio. "Birdhouse Project #5," *l'Arca*, February 1999.

Cook, Hugh. "Angling for a Sharper Image," *Building Design & Construction*, March 1999.

Housely, Laura. "Super Fly Guys, Great Airport Design," *Wallpaper*, June 1999.

Weiser, Nora. "Reflecting a National Image Through Design: The Doha International Airport Competition," *Competitions*, Winter 1998/1999.

Lui, Elizabeth Gill. *Closed Mondays*, published to coincide with the exhibition "Closed Mondays: The Museum as Art Form," at The American Institute of Architects Gallery, Washington, D.C., 1999; Tucson: Nazraeli Press, 1999.

1998
Tyler, Charles. "Green Beauties," *Airport World*, April 1998.

Holt, Nancy. "DIA Takes Off," *Urban Land*, April 1998.

Catinella, Rita F. "Becoming One with Nature," *Contract Design*, July 1998.

"The Sky Line, Casinos Royale," *The New Yorker*, September 14, 1998.

Young, Renée. "Historic Renovation Awards," *Building Design & Construction*, November 1998.

Master Architect Series III: Fentress Bradburn, The Images Publishing Group, December 1998.

Home from Sky: Airport-Designer Designed Birdhouses, Tokyo: The Executive Committee Birdhouse Project, 1998.

Educational Spaces: A Pictorial Review, Volume I, The Images Publishing Group, 1998.

1997
Dubbs, Dana. "Democracy in the Desert," *Facilities Design & Management*, January 1997.

Arnaboldi, Mario Antonio. "National Wildlife Museum," *l'Arca*, February 1997.

Busch, Jennifer Thiele. "Leaving 'Las Vegas'," *Contract Design*, February 1997.

Brooke, James. "Denver's New Airport Flying High," *San Francisco Chronicle*, March 1997.

Webb, Michael. "Denver Airport," *The Architecture of Stations and Terminals*, New York: Arco for Hearst Books International, December 1997.

1996
Mays, Vernon. "Federal Buildings and Campuses," *Architecture*, January 1996.

Arnaboldi, Mario Antonio. "An American in Qatar," *l'Arca*, October 1996.

1995
Egan, Timothy. "A Shrine to Western Wildlife," *The New York Times*, January 29, 1995.

Blake, Edward. "Poetry in Motion," *The Architectural Review*, February 1995.

Vitta, Maurizio. "National Cowboy Hall of Fame," *l'Arca*, April 1995.

Dietsch, Deborah K. "Embracing Landscape," *Architecture*, May 1995.

Collyer, Stanley. "Curtis Fentress," *Competitions*, Fall 1995.

Chandler, Roger. *Fentress Bradburn Architects*, Washington, D.C.: Studio Press (AIA), 1995.

Curtis Worth Fentress, Milan: L'Arca Edizioni, 1995.

1994
Schutt, Craig A. "Fentress Bradburn's Winning Ways Aid Growth," *Ascent*, Spring 1994.

Dubbs, Dana. "The Government Center That Came In On Budget," *Facilities Design and Management*, May 1994.

Bianchi, Walter. "The Natural Resources Building In Olympia Washington," *l'Arca*, May 1994.

Barreneche, Raul A. "Peak Performance," *Architecture*, August 1994.

Kaplan, James. "Now, An Airport You Can Love?," *Condé Nast Traveler*, October 1994.

Russell, James S. "Is This Any Way To Build An Airport?", *Architectural Record*, November 1994.

Pavarini, Stefano. "Denver International Airport," *l'Arca*, November 1994.

Wright, Gordon. "Curved Complex Conveys Distinctive Civic Character," *Building Design & Construction*, December 1994.

1993

"New Seoul Metropolitan Airport," *Progressive Architecture*, March 1993.

Arnaboldi, Mario Antonio. "Airport on the Water," *l'Arca*, May 1993.

Dubbs, Dana. "Easy Breathing in Washington," *Facilities Design and Management*, May 1993.

Dietsch, Deborah K. "Green Realities," *Architecture*, June 1993.

Stein, Karen D. "'Snow Capped' Symbol," *Architectural Record*, June 1993.

Cattaneo, Renato. "A Canopied Air Terminal," *l'Arca*, July/August 1993.

Chandler, Roger, "Variations on a Theme," *Competitions*, Summer, 1993.

1992

Vitta, Maurizio. "National Cowboy Hall of Fame," *l'Arca*, April 1992.

Shaman, Diana. "Seeking Remedies for Indoor Air Pollution Problems," *The New York Times*, April 12, 1992.

Green, Peter. "Big Ain't Hardly the Word For It," *Engineering News Record*, September 1992.

Harriman, Marc S. "Designing for Daylight," *Architecture*, October 1992.

Pierson, John. "Denver Airport Rises Under Gossamer Roof," *The Wall Street Journal*, November 17, 1992.

Chandler, Roger. "Learning from Las Vegas?" *Competitions*, Winter 1992.

1991

"Denver Airport Design Unveiled," *Building Design and Construction,* January 1991.

"Bye, Bye, Dumb Box," *Contract Design*, March 1991.

1990

Stubbs, M. Stephanie. "Civic Facelift," *Architecture*, March 1990.

"Olympia's Natural Resources Building," *Architectural Record,* November 1990.

"Jefferson County Courts and Administration Building," publication for the American Institute of Architects exhibition: "Architecture For Justice," 1990.

1988

Vaughan, Douglas. "Focus Denver: Convention Center Coming," *New York Times,* July 17, 1988.

1987

Cooper, Jerry. "Balboa Company," *Interiors*, August 1987.

1986

Canty, Donald. "Building with a Checkered Past Renovated as a Museum," *Architecture*, November 1986.

1985

Yee, Roger. "A Dream Office for a Denver Oilman," *Corporate Design & Realty*, December 1985.

1984

"The Museum of Western Art," *Interior Design*, October 1984.

Chalmers, Ray. "Mullion-free Exterior Enhances Office Views," *Building Design & Construction*, March 1984.

1983

Creamer, Anita. "Denver's Cosmopolitan Broadway Grill is a Stunning, High-tech Adventure in Downtown Dining," Empire Magazine, *The Denver Post*, January 1983.

1982

"C.W. Fentress Designs Denver's Reliance Center," *Architectural Record*, March 1982.

Acknowledgments

The success of the projects presented in this book was made possible through the efforts of many people, and thanks go to all of our associates and collaborators.
The book itself was a collaborative undertaking. Special thanks go to the following individuals for their contributions: Shawn Turney, Tymmie Serr and Lisa Hillmer for photography and image coordination; Val Moses for writing; and Karen Gilbert, whose broad knowledge of Fentress Bradburn's work was invaluable. This project also reflects the influence of many others, including architects Curt Fentress, Mike Winters, Mark Outman, Ned Kirschbaum, Thom Walsh, Jeff Olson, Brian Chaffee, Deborah Lucking, Derek Starkenburg, Scott Allen, Robin Ault, and Kristoffer Kenton, and information specialist Les Stuart. Their efforts are greatly appreciated.
The firm would also like to thank Alessina Brooks and Paul Latham of The Images Publishing Group for including us in this monograph series and for all their support and guidance throughout the project; Renée Otmar for copy-editing; and Rod Gilbert and Antony Lord of The Graphic Image Studio for their attentive and helpful handling of our material during the production process.

Photography Credits:

Architecture Culture: 32 (23); 33 (25); 34 (1,2)
Patrick Barta: 115; 117 (12)
Milt Borchert: 124 (1,2); 125 (7,8)
Trine Bumiller: 189 (2,4); 190 (6); 191 (9)
Gary Chamer: 190 (7)
Chris Chavez: 180 (3)
Jeff Goldberg, Esto: 53 (2,3); 54 (5); 56 (7); 57 (8–11); 58 (13); 59 (14); 98 (9,11); 99; 101 (16); 104 (23,25); 105 (27); 150 (1,2); 152–153; 154 (6,8); 156 (11); 158 (13); 162 (20,23); 164 (25); 165 (26,27)
Lisa Hillmer: 11 (1); 15 (5); 74 (33); 75 (4,5); 102 (18,19); 103 (21); 118 (1–3); 121 (7)
Greg Hursley: 192 (1,2); 193 (3); 194 (5); 195 (6,7)
Timothy Hursley: 96 (5); 100 (14); 102 (17); 103 (22); 105 (26); 106 (29,31); 108 (34); 109; 110 (39); 111 (40,41,43); 151 (3); 154 (7); 159 (15); 161; 162 (22); 166 (1,2); 167 (4); 168 (6); 169; 172–173
Ron Johnson: 12 (3); 47 (2); 48 (3); 61; 91 (2,4); 92 (6); 176 (3); 179 (6); 181 (4); 182; 183 (6)
Nick Merrick/Hedrich-Blessing: 18 (1); 20; 21 (4); 22 (7); 23 (8); 24 (9); 25 (10); 26 (12,13); 27; 28; 30 (19); 31; 32 (21,22,24); 35 (3,4); 36 (5,6); 37; 38–39; 40 (9); 41; 60 (15); 75 (6,9); 76 (10); 77 (11,13); 90 (1); 92 (7); 93; 106 (30); 108 (33); 111 (42); 112 (1); 114 (6,7); 116; 117 (11); 120; 121 (6,8); 122 (9,10,11,12,13); 135 (4); 136 (6); 138; 141; 157; 158 (14); 160 (17,18); 162 (21); 164 (24); 168 (8); 170 (11,12); 171 (13,14); 174; 175 (18,19); 181 (5); 183 (7); 184 (2); 186 (5–7); 196 (1–3); 197 (4,5); 199 (2–5)
John Miller: 177 (4); 178, 179 (7); 185 (4)
Robert Reck: 166 (3)
Wes Thompson: 13 (4)

Rendering Credits:

Robin Ault: 46 (1)
Carl Dalio: 51 (12,13); 67 (19–21); 184 (1); 189 (3); 213 (7); 220 (1); 222 (7); 223 (12–14)
Kling Lindquist: 84 (7,8); 85 (9,10); 86 (11); 87 (12)

Model Credits:

Lisa Hillmer: 215 (9–12)
Ron Johnson: 50 (6–11); 62 (2–6); 63 (7,8); 64 (11); 65 (12); 66 (13–18); 80 (1); 82 (3); 83 (4,5); 89 (2–7); 91 (3); 96 (1–4); 97 (7); 113 (3); 126 (1); 127 (4); 130 (8,9); 132 (1); 133 (3–5); 134 (2,3); 140 (10,11); 146 (6,7); 147 (10,11); 206 (1); 207 (2–5); 212 (2–5); 214 (1–4); 216 (2); 218 (5–7); 221 (3); 222 (6); 223 (10,11)
Will Moore: 205 (3)

Non-credited images: courtesy Fentress Bradburn Architects

Index

Bold numbers represent projects featured in Selected and Current Works

116 Inverness Drive East 232
1800 Grant Street 233
1999 Broadway 14, 232
3790 Howard Hughes Parkway **134**, 246
3883 Howard Hughes Parkway **134**, 229, 243
3993 Howard Hughes Parkway **134**, 229, 245
421 Broadway Renovation/Expansion **74**, 248
809 Olive Way 238

AEC Design Competition 1996, The **142**, 229, 244
Air Zoo at Kalamazoo 249
associates and collaborators 227
awards 230

Balboa Company Corporate Headquarters, The **196**, 234
Bank Lofts, The 244
Birdhouse Project 1998, The **202**, 246
Black American West Museum 230, 236
Blackhawk Casino 246
Boise Civic Center 237
Bradburn, James Henry 13, 14, 227
Bronco Stadium 247
Buffalo Bill Historical Center 246

Capitol Area - East End Campus 249
Capitol Tower/J.D. Tower 233
Castlewood Plaza Master Plan 235
Catalina Resort Community 240
Cathedral City Civic Center **144**, 243
Cathedral Square 239
Centennial Office Park Master Plan 235
Central California History Museum **216**, 248
Cherry Creek Plaza 237
Cherry Creek South Condominiums 248
Cherry Hills Community Church Chapel **88**, 249
Citibank/Citicorp Diners Club 246
City of Oakland Administration Building 229, 230, 243
Civic Center Parking Structure **124**, 229, 247
Clark County Government Center 9, 14, 34, **96**, 229, 230, 241
Clark County Master Plan 241
Colorado Christian Home/Tennyson Center for Children and Families 242
Colorado Christian University **220**, 248
Colorado Convention Center 11, 14, 229, 230, 237
Colorado Convention Center Expansion **46**, 249
Colorado Convention Center Hotel 240
Colorado History Museum Expansion **214**, 249
Colorado School of Mines 236
Colorado State Capitol Life-Safety Renovation **70**, 238, 249
competitions 229
Complex Suria Merdeka (Kuching Town Centre) **78**, 245
Coors Field 240
Crystal Center 232

Data General Field Engineering Logistics Center 229, 235
David E. Skaggs Federal Building 9, **52**, 241
David Eccles Conference Center and Peery's Egyptian Theater 241
Deira Bus Station and Car Park 246
Denver Academy 247
Denver Art Museum 237
Denver Central Library and Urban Analysis 238
Denver International Airport Passenger Terminal 12, 14, **166**, 230, 239
Denver Permit Center, The **176**, 237
DIA Westin Hotel 244
Dinosaur Discovery Museum **212**, 230, 240
Dixon, John Morris 11–15
Dunbar Resort, The 243

Eastbank Conference Center and Hotel 240
Englewood Mixed-Use Center 234
Estes Park Community and Conference Center 238

Fentress, Curtis Worth 9, 13, 14, 15, 18, 96, 102, 202, 227
Fiddler's Green Amphitheater 236
Fiddler's Green Center Building II 248
Flughafen Wien (Vienna Airport Expansion) **132**, 248
Franklin and Lake 237

Goldrush Casino 246
Greenville Park Tower 235
Gulf Canada Resources Ltd **198**, 244
Gunter Hall Renovation 242

Hawaii Convention Center 242
Holy Ghost Roman Catholic Church 233
Hughes Center, The **134**, 229, 243, 245, 246

IBM Customer Service Center **192**, 239
ICE Terminal Köln-Deutz/Messe **204**, 248
ICG Communications Corporate Headquarters 244
Idaho Power Company Corporate Headquarters, 236

J.D. Edwards & Co. Corporate Campus **90**, 244
Janus Corporate Campus 249
Jefferson County Government Center Courts and Administration Building 237
Jefferson County Government Center Master Plan, 236
Jefferson County Human Services Building 230, 236

Kittredge Building 232
Kuala Lumpur Airport 240
Kuala Lumpur Hotel and Office Complex 245
Kuwait Finance House Tower **42**, 248
Kwangju Bank Headquarters 241

La Nueva Área Terminal del Aeropuerto Madrid/Barajas **126**, 245
Larimer County Justice Center **118**, 124, 229, 246
Lexington Center 235
Loveland Police and Courts Building **68**, 249
Lucent Technologies 247

Madrid/Barajas Technical Services 247
M-E Engineers Building 248
Midway Office Complex and Master Plan 245
Milestone Square Master Plan 232
Milestone Tower 232
Montrose Government Center 242
Moscow Redevelopment Project 240
Mountain Bell Special Services Center 235
Museum of Western Art/The Navarre 230–231, 233

National Cowboy Hall of Fame Renovation/Expansion 14, 229, 240
National Museum of Wildlife Art 11, **150**, 229, 231, 239
Natural Resources Building **112**, 229, 231, 238
New Doha International Airport, The 229, 245
Norwest Tower 235

Odd Fellows Hall 233
One DTC 234
One Mile High Plaza 232
One Polo Creek 242
One Wynkoop Plaza 243
Oxbridge Town Center 237

Palmetto Bay Beach Resort **188**, 245
Parkway Plaza Master Plan 235
Peery's Egyptian Theater 231, 241
Pioneer Plaza Hotel 235
Presidio Town Center 246

Reconstruction of the Souks of Beirut: An International Ideas Competition, The 242
Regional Transportation Commission and Regional Flood Control District Headquarters **34**, 231, 245
Reliance Tower 233
Republic Park Hotel 234
Research Complex I (University of Colorado Health Sciences Center) **80**, 247
Ronstadt Transit Center 15, 231, 236

Sacramento High Rise Lot A **206**, 249
Seattle-Tacoma International Airport Central Terminal Expansion **62**, 247
Second Bangkok International Airport 241
Seoul Inchon International Airport Passenger Terminal 9, **18**, 229, 243
Smith, Brooks, Bolshoun & Co. 247
Southbridge One 232
Southbridge Plaza 233
Sun Plaza 236

Tele-Communications, Inc., Headquarters 234
Temple Sinai **184**, 234
Terminal 2, Flughafen München (Second Terminal, Munich Airport) **208**, 245
Terrace Building 232
Terrace Towers Master Plan 232
Tritch Building Renovation and The Rialto Café, The **180**, 231, 244
Tucson City Center Master Plan 234

Union Station Redevelopment Plan 239
University Art Museum 239
University of Colorado Mathematics Building/Gemmill Engineering Library 231, 238

Vladivostok City Center 241

Welton Street Parking Garage 233
West Hills Hotel, 240
Westlake Residences 238

YMCA 234

Every effort has been made to trace the original source of copyright material contained in this book. The publishers would be pleased to hear from copyright holders to rectify any errors or omissions.

The information and illustrations in this publication have been prepared and supplied by Fentress Bradburn Architects. While all reasonable efforts have been made to ensure accuracy, the publishers do not, under any circumstances, accept responsibility for errors, omissions and representations express or implied.

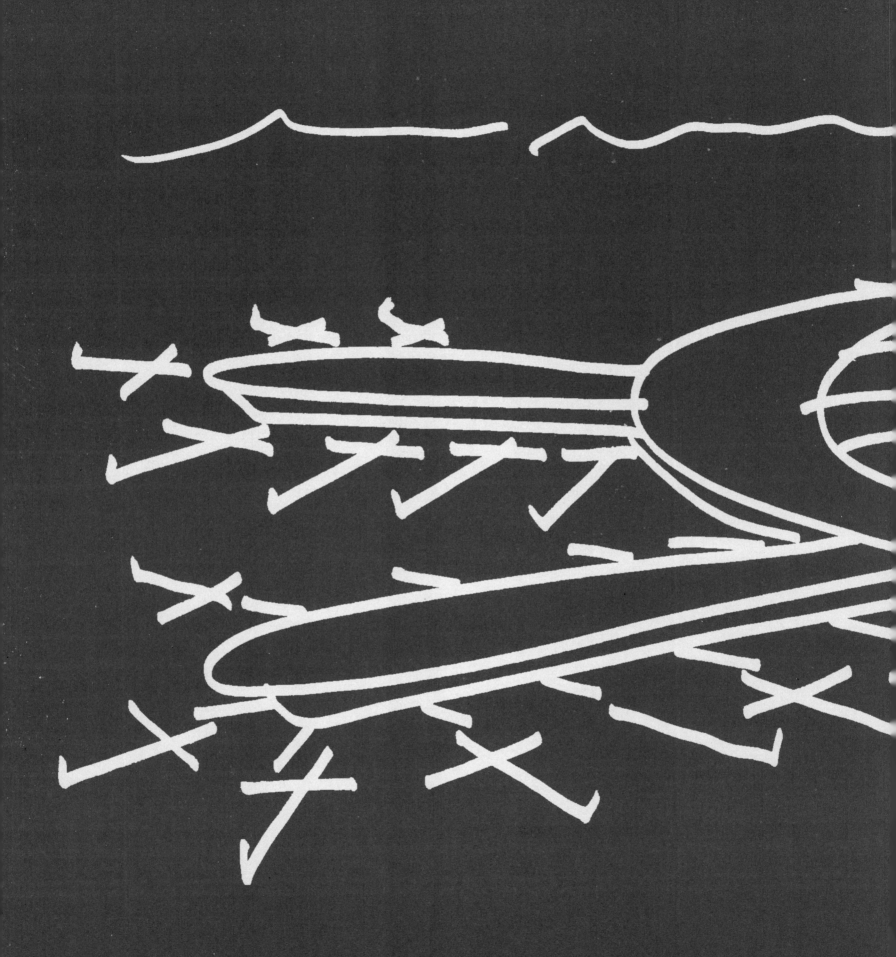